Essay Index

POETS AT PRAYER

POETS
AT PRAYER

by

Sister Mary James Power, S.S.N.D.

Essay Index Reprint Series

BOOKS FOR LIBRARIES PRESS
FREEPORT, NEW YORK

LIBRARY OF CONGRESS CATALOG CARD NUMBER:

68-29239

PRINTED IN THE UNITED STATES OF AMERICA

NIHIL OBSTAT
Michael F. Dinneen, S.S., D.D.
Censor Librorum

IMPRIMATUR
Michael J. Curley, D.D.
Archbishop of Baltimore

BALTIMORE, OCTOBER 10, 1938.

To
MY MOTHER
and
MY FATHER

TABLE OF CONTENTS

x   **Contents**

ACKNOWLEDGMENTS

THE making of any book is a long and arduous process. Seldom is it a personal one. There are many, then, who have contributed, through their enthusiasm and advice, to the preparation of this book. And they are respected gratefully.

The author owes special thanks to her religious order, the School Sisters of Notre Dame, who gave her time and opportunity to study; to Reverend Fr. Frederick J. Mulrey, Pastor of St. Thomas' Church, Millis, Mass., for many discussions on the philosophical problems involved; to Mr. John J. Reynolds, Medford, Mass., booklover, whose patient search for rare editions was tireless; to Dr. James E. Tobin, Head of the English Department, Fordham University, Graduate School, for advice and supervision; to Dr. Henry W. Wells, Professor of English, Columbia University, for his courtesy in writing the Foreword; to Mr. John L. Foley, friend, companion, and literary executor of the poet, Thomas S. Jones, Jr., whose reciprocal love for poetry and for the saints first inspired this work.

She wishes also to make due acknowledgment to the authorities of Fordham University for permission to use much of the material included in this book, material which was originally employed in papers presented to the faculty during the course of graduate study.

She is particularly grateful to the poets themselves for their generous-spiritedness toward repeated questions and frequent letters and for their gracious consent to permit their "revelations" to be exposed.

She wishes to express her sincere gratitude to those

who have generously given permission to reprint selections from the works of the poets included in this book:

Brandt & Brandt for quotations from the works of Edna St. V. Millay: *The Buck in the Snow,* published by Harper & Brothers (copyright, 1928, by Edna St. Vincent Millay); *Renascence and Other Poems,* published by Harper & Brothers (copyright, 1917, by Edna St. Vincent Millay); *Second April,* published by Harper & Brothers (copyright, 1921, by Edna St. Vincent Millay); *Harp Weaver and Other Poems,* published by Harper & Brothers (copyright, 1920, 1921, 1922, 1923, by Edna St. Vincent Millay); *Fatal Interview,* published by Harper & Brothers (copyright, 1931, by Edna St. Vincent Millay).

Mr. Robert P. T. Coffin, Brunswick, Me., for quotations from *Dew and Bronze,* published by A. & C. Boni.

The Commonweal, New York, for selections from *The Housing of the Lambs,* by Robert P. Tristram Coffin, and *The Startled Heron,* by Robert P. Tristram Coffin.

Mr. John L. Foley, New York, for selections from *Shadow of the Perfect Rose, Collected Poems of Thomas S. Jones, Jr.,* published by Farrar and Rinehart, New York.

Harcourt, Brace and Co., Inc., New York, for quotations from: *Collected Poems of T. S. Eliot*; *The Rock,* by T. S. Eliot; *Ash Wednesday,* by T. S. Eliot. Also to Faber and Faber for permission to reprint these same selections.

Alfred A. Knopf, Inc., New York, authorized publishers, for special arrangement to use selections from *Collected Poems of Elinor Wylie.*

Macmillan Co. for selections from the following: *The Yoke of Thunder,* by Robert P. Tristram Coffin; *The Golden Falcon,* by Robert P. Tristram Coffin; *Strange*

Holiness, by Robert P. Tristram Coffin. *Collected Poems of Vachel Lindsay. Collected Poems of John Masefield; Coming of Christ,* by John Masefield; also to Mr. John Masefield for permission to reprint the same selections. *Collected Poems of Edwin Arlington Robinson; Cavender's House,* by Edwin Arlington Robinson; *Sonnets,* by Edwin Arlington Robinson; *The Glory of the Nightingales,* by Edwin Arlington Robinson; *Matthias at the Door,* by Edwin Arlington Robinson; *Nicodemus,* by Edwin Arlington Robinson; *Talifer,* by Edwin Arlington Robinson; *Amaranth,* by Edwin Arlington Robinson.

Mr. Edwin Markham, New York, for selections from: *The Man with the Hoe, Lincoln and Other Poems, Shoes of Happiness, The Gates of Paradise,* and *New Poems,* published by Doubleday, Doran, New York; *My Religion,* published by New Church Messenger.

Houghton, Mifflin Company, Boston, Mass., for selections from: *The Heart of the Road,* by Anna Hempstead Branch; *Rose of the Wind,* by Anna Hempstead Branch; *The Shoes That Danced,* by Anna Hempstead Branch; *Sonnets from a Lock Box,* by Anna Hempstead Branch.

Oxford University Press, London, England, for quotations from: *Poems of Conformity,* by Charles Williams; *Windows of the Night,* by Charles Williams; *Divorce,* by Charles Williams; also to Charles Williams for permission to reprint these same selections.

Random House, New York, for quotations from: *Dear Judas,* by Robinson Jeffers; *Thurso's Landing,* by Robinson Jeffers; *The Women at Point Sur,* by Robinson Jeffers; *Give Your Heart to the Hawks,* by Robinson Jeffers.

Charles Scribner's Sons, New York, for quotations from

the works of John Hall Wheelock: *Dust and Light; The Black Panther; The Bright Doom.*

Sheed and Ward, New York City, for quotations from: *The Unknown God,* by Alfred Noyes.

Frederick A. Stokes Company for quotations from: *The Lord of Misrule,* by Alfred Noyes; *Collected Poems,* 3 vols., by Alfred Noyes.

PREFACE

IT IS the purpose of the pages which follow to discover the attitude toward religion of some of the generally acknowledged leaders in contemporary English and American Poetry. The study is an objective one. The author is, of course, at variance with those beliefs contrary to the tenets of her own Faith. She has merely endeavored to find out from the poets themselves what they believe concerning God and man's relations with God.

Poetry had birth in the first recorded words, "Let there be light!", which came from Supreme Intelligence, Imagination, Emotion, and Truth, from the Creator of the cadence of the solar system and of interstellar space. As Deity Itself personifies poetry, great poetry leads to and from God, the Spirit of Truth. Accordingly, it deals with the wonders of the inner life. It draws from the wellsprings of man's heart and spirit.

As life continues to call for poetry, the poets go on with the traditional themes: they are still singing their relations with God. By nature they have always been the discoverers, the probers, the high-priests of truth. Instinctively, they pour out the fullness of their heart in homage to the Source of Eternal Truth. Percy Mackaye writes that

> . . . the expression of his 'relation to the Unknown' is the *raison d'être* of the work of every sincere artist. It is certainly the reason for the expression of what is best in my own work.

Whether one accepts John Cowper Powys' definition of religion,

> Religion is the life urge concentrated upon the mystery behind life;

or that of Rose Macaulay,

> Religion is a belief in extranatural agencies with whom
> the believer thinks he can establish some kind of personal
> relation;

or that of Ridgely Torrence,

> Religion is any individual's consciousness of and relation
> to infinite being or to any aspect of it which appears to
> him as his highest ideal;

or the Catholic theological interpretation of religion,

> The combination of truths and offices by which our life
> is directed to God;

the constant quantity in each is a superior Being to whom
man feels he owes worship; the variable is man's fulfillment of his relations with the object of his belief. Yet in
all the attitudes, religion is a voluntary habit of the mind,
through which habit man, knowing that something repre-
sents the Highest Intelligence, intuitively offers homage.

In centuries past, among the seers of truth and beauty,
there have been those blessed with a clarity of vision, high
faith, and the grace to surrender their wills and hearts to
the Mystery of Love.

Some there have been who, as Edwin Arlington Robinson writes, cannot accept the tenets of any church. "Religion for them is a thing for each to find or feel for himself." Uncertainty and a changing age has made them, as
Arnold has it, wanderers

> . . . between two worlds, the one dead,
> The other powerless to be born.

Others, again, have turned to pagan references for truth
and have taken refuge in words like "Fate," "One Being,"
or the "One Self."

With the first group, whom we have called the seers,—
Francis Thompson, Alice Meynell, Lionel Johnson, and
Louise Guiney,—we shall not be concerned. They have
assurance; their belief coincides with the teachings of the
Catholic Church. Rather shall we regard those poets whose
work reveals a varying sense of creed.

It is not only difficult, useless, and somewhat painful to
classify contemporary poets into specific schools or sects,
it is likewise unacceptable to the poets themselves. As
Perry writes:

> Some deeply religious poets would hesitate to identify
> themselves with any church, but nevertheless they may
> be 'in spirit and in truth,' men of profound religious
> instincts.

Yet for the purpose of examination, they can be placed,
without too Procrustean a torture, in three groups: pagans
or lovers of earthly beauty, puzzled seekers after God, and
those naturally Christian.

The "pagans" are those who give earth their all, who
leave it only to go to heaven, as Robert Frost says, "by
"climbing a birch tree," secretly hoping that the branches
will soon rebound to place them safely again at the feet of
Mother Earth. They acknowledge an overruling power
controlling the known universe as well as the unknown.
In no sense is that power a personal God. It is the Great
Unknowable of the Intellect, as held by the agnostics, who
maintain that human reason can never arrive at a knowledge of God; it is the God of pantheism which identifies
matter, energy, and man with Divinity; it is that rigid unknown force which predetermines the destiny of humanity; or it is the avenging God of the deists, who disregard
Divine Providence, revelation, and Christianity.

To these various deities some of the contemporary poets give credence. Dissimilar in their pagan attitudes, they are similar in their inconsistency.

Among them may be placed:

John Hall Wheelock, an agnostic, professedly yet unwillingly so; whose idea of God is uncertain, accepting the idea of One Pattern in the world to which all conform blindly, One Rhythm, which holds all in uniform restraint, One Spirit, in sympathy with all creation, but obsessing man with wonder, doubt, grief, as well as worship—a system of negation under which Wheelock struggles constantly, his believing heart at war with his unbelieving mind; from which he tries to escape into Nirvana.

Edna St. Vincent Millay, whose god is beauty, surrendering herself to which she reaches a kind of spirituality; a spirituality, however, which is no more than an elevation of spirit or of the emotions which serves as an escape from her despairing self; despairing, because earth means all and heaven nothing, earth is complete in itself, and yet so empty, so full of dust, that there is little more than gloom; gloom which, in later years, is a lament for beauty, a grief for love.

Elinor Wylie, the perfection of pagan stoicism; an adamant soul, who never allowed her imaginative mind to bestir her apathetic heart; unlike Millay in that she followed the lore of Artemis rather than that of Venus, like her in her awareness of dust; in later years, a period of transition through agnosticism, in her posthumous work, revelation of a belief in immortality, death as a refuge, not as a stern destroyer.

John Masefield, who believes in the crisscross of circumstances determined by Fate, inevitable, supreme, yet providing an everlasting mercy which reconciles man's misgivings as to a propitious end; not believing in the City of God, but expressing the feeling that it will never be reached; now holding to transmigration; now asserting that man touches God everywhere, that men have the power of God, that there is nothing but brotherhood; a fatalist, an immanentist, a pantheist.

Robinson Jeffers, both pantheist and deist, the one at opposite poles from the other, holding at once total annihilation and its impossibility; a destructive voice picturing man as a pawn in the hands of an avenging Deity; picturing also God revealed through man's action.

Next there are those who are definitely "seekers after truth," possessed of a consciousness of God, of a personal God at times, even of Christ, generally of a Provident Good that directs their ends and of which they seek a fuller understanding.

Here may be placed:

Edwin Arlington Robinson, charged by some as an agnostic and a fatalist, but championed here as one, as he said himself, who could not find his way; who said that there is no man who believes nothing; who followed a flickering flame of faith which lighted up home in a God Who guides and guards men, a God Whose ways are omnipotent, inscrutable to man, Who leads men to the conclusion that death is a beginning and not an end.

Edwin Markham, prophet of "the kingdom coming," believer in the brotherhood of man founded on the law of love personified in Christ.

Vachel Lindsay, like Markham a follower of Swedenborg, to a certain extent; similarly a prophet and evangelist, pointing out to man the joy of living with love and with beauty, the joy of redemption, and the joy of resurrection.

Robert P. Tristram Coffin, seeking permanent vision in a world whose beauty he believes to have been created by a Supreme and Infinite Personal Being he calls God. He sees God apart from these created things; fleeting conceptions of pantheism however recur.

Finally there are those who are poets "naturally Christian," celebrating in their songs the essential truths of Christian, sometimes even of Catholic, belief.

Here belong such figures as:

Alfred Noyes, who, once harassed by doubts inspired by Darwin, Huxley, Haeckel, and Spencer, has emerged from the struggle by an intuitive faith; who concludes that life, wonderful beyond man's comprehension, necessarily professes a Greater Intelligence for its being; who lives for the sake of love, desiring only what would chasten his spirit; who sings of the Resurrection of man, the Justice of God, His Providence, and the shadow of the Cross as the gift of Peace.

T. S. Eliot, who has emerged out of a waste-land of doubt, through a soul-rending spiritual evolution, to an inheritance he has accepted with great humility of heart, to a belief in redemption, in immortality, in the Communion of the Saints, in the Divinity of Christ and the Virginity of Mary.

Charles Williams, like Eliot, of the Church of England, whose theme is love everlasting, a love embracing the whole world, making all men brothers; beside which intellectual love there stands the "scala sancta," which he ascends through nuptial love, as did Coventry Patmore.

Anna Hempstead Branch, loving mankind practically,

as a settlement worker; poetically, as a philanthropist of the poor, the wan, the ruined; strong of voice against the social oppressor, worker in symbols, ·which lead to the acceptance of the Trinity, Purgatory, penance, Christ as the Light and the Redeemer of the world; mystic, in that some of her songs show her inebriated with the Presence of Love.

Thomas S. Jones, Jr., to whom love was the Kingdom of the Holy Ghost, who sang always of the Perfect City, seeking beauty in the shining sanctity of God, perceiving truth in Christ the Perfect Lover, in the saints, the martyrs of Love; expounding its dogma, the attributes of Christ, the Immaculate Conception, the Virgin Birth, the Passion of Christ and its significance; like Charles Williams, celebrating its feast days with an abundance of music.

Love, these feel, as did St. Thomas, is more unifying than knowledge. Indeed, it is the vital principle of their existence. They believe that they will be judged at last on the merits of their love for God and for their fellowmen. As the virtues of a piece of art manifest the virtues of its maker, so the songs of these poets naturally Christian are of the essence of that Paradise long lost and long sought by the human heart, "Love . . . the kingdom of the Holy Ghost."

Baltimore,   SISTER MARY JAMES, PH.D.
November 30, 1938

FOREWORD

THERE is a language of religion and a language of philosophy. In theology the two grow interrelated. On one extreme, that of religion becomes most itself in ritual and homily; that of philosophy, in logic and disputation. Distinguished from both, but at times merging with each, is the language of art and poetry. The aesthetic imagination is not in itself that of religion or philosophy, but it is a brother to them and on the whole friendly. The three often converse together in the high consistory of the mind. Sometimes the aesthetic imagination seems the youngest brother, the most tender and beautiful, with childlike countenance and without the austerities of his companions. Sometimes he seems oldest of all, descended from a dim and primitive age, and he feels the affection for his companions which an older brother experiences who has watched over the growth and cared lovingly for the education of his fellows.

From the most primitive times religion has called upon beauty to be her support, and beauty in turn has leaned upon religion. From the earliest times, too, philosophy, as it has grown warm and human, has found expression in poetry and art. The earliest fragments of the thinkers are in verse; the earliest poems are hymns. Nor is this merely a primitive condition. So far as we can see, it belongs equally to the present and the future. As I write these words of detached criticism, hundreds of ardent spirits are bent upon the task of painting, carving, or fashioning in words the images of their thoughts upon life and the universe, the symbols of their faith, their belief, and their devotion. No man can envisage the beginning or foresee the end of such activity.

Although the present age seems a declining one for the poets, writers of verse as well as of inspired prose are still giving expression to man's experiences in his search for the unity and purpose of life. Some of the rarest and most lyrical moments of this adventure are captured today in verse. The writers of such poetry do not make the greatest stir in the present world, but theirs is a still, small voice, which it is folly, and that high, totally to disregard. The philosophers should hear them, religious men and women should hear them, and, ideally speaking, we should all hear them.

Those of us who have read to any extent in the literature of the last century, especially that of England, breathe a sigh of relief that the heat of the spiritual struggles of that particular age is over. We have struggles of our own, more vital to us and no less stirring but on the whole distinctly less distressing. During that era men's hearts were touched to the quick, especially in countries where Protestantism predominated. Much of the thinking, as represented in *In Memoriam,* for example, now seems to us crude. The mishandling of transcendental themes often smacked of adolescent melancholy and vague spiritual desire. We at least imagine ourselves as gradually outgrowing these attitudes. But a complete materialism and absence of speculation or of definite faith is perhaps even more deplorable than the muddled doubt and muddled faith of very many of our ancestors. Nor is such shallowness seriously threatening our civilization as a whole. As I have already said, life as conceived by the synthetic and poetic imagination still continues to be the object of speculation, the subject of belief. Since the World War there has been a greatly increased interest in so-called metaphysical poetry. The works of Donne, Herbert, Vaughan,

Crashaw, and Traherne have been the objects of vastly increased attention. English scholars have recovered the true meaning of their great medieval religious poem, *Piers Plowman*. We have celebrated the six-hundredth anniversary of the death of the most deathless of all philosophical poets, Dante.

It is appropriate and timely, therefore, that Sister Mary James should write a study of the English and American poets of the last twenty years who have contemplated most effectively the ultimate issues of life and faith. Urania, the heavenly Muse, did not weep herself to death over the body of Keats, nor of Francis Thompson. Though capable of pain, as Shelley wrote, she is immortal. And she is with us still. As fancy leads us to think of a perpetual music in heaven, so there is sacred music always on earth. Some of it is faltering, through affected aestheticism or shallow speculation or inadequate conviction. Not all the poets whom Sister Mary James discusses so sympathetically in her book are equally distinguished as artists or as thinkers. But all are significant. And it is perhaps worth noting that the poets who inherit the querulous attitude of the typical Victorians appear today the least distinguished. Those who have written best in our own century have had at least a positive tone. Thomas Hardy's *Dynasts* states a naturalistic philosophy no less frankly than Mr. T. S. Eliot's *Murder in the Cathedral* states the Catholic position. And certainly one of the most brilliant poets represented in the present volume, the late Thomas S. Jones, Jr., came far more happily than the lugubrious Mr. Eliot to the position of the worshiper. America has had her characteristic saints, tarnished, perhaps, but none the less sincere. Several of them are recorded in this book, as Vachel Lindsay and Anna Hempstead Branch. She has had, too, her stirring and picturesque idealists, as Edwin Markham and Robert P. T. Coffin. England, as this survey discloses, produces more mature but less colorful seers in spiritual song.

The survey by Sister Mary James will be found, I think, original in its critical point of view and inspiring alike to lovers of poetry, of philosophy, and of Christ. It will be best understood by those who love all three.

HENRY W. WELLS, PH.D.

Columbia University, New York City

INTRODUCTION:

What the Nineteenth Century poets believed

THE nineteenth century, like most centuries, was the repository of the beliefs of the immediate, as well as the remote past. Like most ages, which fail to heed or perhaps to understand the mistakes of their ancestors, it took over almost without question the ills of the eighteenth century and acquired many more of its own. Protest against authority, civil and religious, had marked English thought since the Reformation and the Renaissance. In the midst of this inheritance: the rationalism of Shaftesbury, the evangelism of Wesley, and the radicalism of the contemporary cult of Godwin, there arose conflict. Even the adherents of the orthodox tradition did not escape chaos. Doubt harassed them as it did the little College of Twelve. And some who had been born in the direct light of truth now received it in refracted rays.

The Reign of Terror was the final aggravation before the political and social upheaval of the nineteenth century. It had propagated the *Zeitgeist*: belief in the trinity of individualism: Liberty, Equality, Fraternity. The Platonic dream of the Lakists was a further development. But as, during the Renaissance, England maintained her self-respect through the national drama, again the spirit of a national consciousness dominated England. Wordsworth, who thought it heaven to be young in the days of revolution, would have the evening star as the emblem of his country.

While social injustice and the consequent oppression of the poor were relieved through measures of parliamentary reform, the poets awoke the national conscience. As a light in a changing age, they were romanticists. Conver-

sion was to be effected through love: by feeling as opposed
to cold, didactic reasoning. Wordsworth was the high-
priest of the gospel of nature. His meditative soul sang
of the familiar wherein he found the supernatural. All
nature had happiness in being. Who does not know of
Wordsworth's faith in believing that every flower enjoys
the very air it breathes? One remembers, too, his insinua-
tion of pre-existence. Yet, apart from both influences,
T. S. Eliot thinks

> . . . there is, in his poetry and in his Preface, a profound
> revival, an inspiration communicated rather to Pusey and
> Newman, to Ruskin, and the great humanitarians, than
> to the accredited poets of the next age.

In conflict with Wordsworth's belief in the relation
of man with nature and with God, were Shelley and
Byron. Yet, they were incarnations of the *Zeitgeist*. But
in their prodigality of freedom, their liberalism, and their
individualism, they outcaptained their captains of romanticism. Their subjectivism and protest defeated their own
purpose. Each knew exile. Self-styled "tameless, swift and
proud," Shelley professed himself an atheist. This is the
youthful Shelley:

> Religion and morality, as they now stand, compose a
> practical code of misery and servitude: the genius of
> human happiness must tear every leaf from the accursed
> book of God ere man can read the inscription on his heart.

Note the pettiness of this gesture of "religion":

> We owe the greatest writers of the golden age of our
> literature to that fervid awakening of the public mind
> which shook to dust the oldest and most oppressive form
> of the Christian religion.

Coleridge speculated upon the metaphysical. And he

so projected his personality that he easily familiarized the supernatural and won willing suspension of belief. Materialism never reached his heart. He kept it in the outer court. If he did play infidel after he had read Voltaire's *Dictionary,* he confessed that the infidel vanity never touched his heart. In America Coleridge and Carlyle had their adherents. German mysticism and French sociology were militating against the Puritanicalism of Puritanism. Amos Bronson Alcott, dean of the Concord School of Philosophy, to which Emerson, Thoreau, Ripley, Parker, and Margaret Fuller belonged, declared himself a transcendentalist when he said:

> I am God. I am greater than God. God is one of my ideas. I therefore contain God; greater is the container than the contained. Therefore, I am greater than God.

It was in the Victorian era that the "honest doubt" of the Cartesians finally triumphed. Science gave with one hand; she took away with the other. The individual was lost in the mass; humanitarianism was the *Summum Bonum.* Romanticism, as an ideal, had been sacrificed on the altar of material progress. Conversions would follow with the reformation in industry and scientific discovery; the din of machines and the wail of the workers would be more comprehensive for reform than Wordsworth's lyric,

> He labors good on good to fix, and owes
> To virtue every triumph that he knows.

There was a reformation. The magic of machinery and the marvels of science made man God, while the turmoil over *The Origin of Species* removed all need of a deity. Tennyson, a Keats in his youth, turned with the tide to an England possessed by the Devil of Doubt and the God of Material Progress. Her wanderings in darkness were his and he cries:

> Chaos, Cosmos! Cosmos, Chaos! who can tell how all will end.

His *In Memoriam* is the *Odyssey* of his soul. Faltering where he had firmly trodden, he inquired the keeper of all the creeds and then defined the age with

> There lives more faith in honest doubt,
> Believe me, than in half the creeds.

But doubt receded. Hope rose to the prospect of belief, lifting him from the mire of half-kinship with the brute to the Mount of Faith where he could vision Hallam living in the God whom Tennyson hoped to see when he had crossed the bar. And with that latter thought, he closed his book in Faith. His credo is, furthermore, in the *Idylls* with all the liturgy of symbolism: the conflict between sense and soul, the Ideal and the Real, the passions and restraint; the strength of purity; and the power of prayer.

Browning's optimism outshone all doubt. In the controversy between religion and science, in the noise of industrialism, he was with Disraeli, on the side of the angels. With implicit belief in the Providence of God and His everlasting mercy for man, Browning exalted human endeavor. The means to the end was sufficient. Aspiration was his ladder to perfection.

The inertia of doubt stands fixed in Arnold. A stoic, he begged "The will to neither strive nor cry." Neither did he dream nor despair. To him, as with all men, life was a warfare. But with his vision, it was fought in the night with ignorant foes. All through his fabric is the dull pattern of

> Wandering between two worlds, one dead,
>   The other powerless to be born,
>   With nowhere yet to rest my head.

T. S. Eliot, in *The Use of Poetry,* attributes to Arnold "only an impeccable demeanor," for he was neither a reactionary nor a rebel. His departure from poetry into prose gave him entrée to himself. His doctrine became "Sweetness and Light." It was Arnoldian culture: the pursuit of perfection, his religious theory. This pursuit of perfection was *in totum*: the fulfillment of the whole man and of all men. There was to be a cooperation of all men to work together unto good in their moral and social zeal to "let reason and the Will of God prevail." Culture then was not only a substitute for religion, because it went farther than religion. But Arnold meant the religion of the nineteenth century. In making culture the pursuit of perfection, in his education of the whole man as well as man *en masse*, he aimed at drawing England from the monopoly of materialism and the god of the Philistines.

Meredith and Hardy were alike and at variance in creed. Both departed from Deity and capitalized Earth and Nature. Meredith was the master of his own fate, the captain of his soul. Intellect was the Absolute. Hardy was the fatalist, poetizing man's behavior as directed by inevitable forces that hold out "A tragical To Be." Meredith wrote his credo in "Never is Earth misread by brain"; Hardy, his personality in

> . . . his nearing death,
> So mocked humanity that she shamed to prize
> A world conditioned thus, or care for breath
> Where Nature such dilemmas could devise.

Protest, we say, was the earmark of the century. The

most soul-stirring one was made against the most sacred
institution of England: her Anglicanism. One of its adherents, John Henry Newman, was the protagonist of the
revolt, the Oxford Movement. It has, as special emphasis,
the illegitimacy of the hierarchy of the Established Church.
As a result, religion, which had dwindled under the
growth of science, became renascent. Many former sup-
porters of Anglicanism, including Newman, entered the
open door of the Roman Catholic Church as the custodian
of orthodoxy. The little red sanctuary lamp was the light
he was seeking amid the encircling gloom. And in this
regeneration of the spirit, poetry, always at home with
religion, ascended not to the level of pure religious belief
but higher, to the Mount of the Transfiguration, to the
tradition of Dante, Petrarch, Southwell, Traherne,
Vaughan, Crashaw, and Blake.

The poets of the orthodox protest were all at peace
with God. Faith, they felt, was a free gift of God. They
triumphed in it as they did in the Love of the Giver.
Love leads to the glory of the Beloved. And in the poets,
the praise comes from their singing angels. Newman had
been led into prose through controversy and apology. But
it is prose on the wing. When his heart was full of the
joy, content, calm, and self-possession that comes from a
sense of refuge in God, he sang in canticle of spiritual
refreshment and a sense of saintliness. In *The Dream of
Gerontius* he seems favored with revelation.

The great poets who followed in the path of the Oxford
Movement are a trinity of inspiration. They walk hand
in hand in the Presence of God: Coventry Patmore, Alice
Meynell, and Francis Thompson. Patmore reached sanctity through nuptial love. A deep spirituality refined natural love to that degree of unification with Supreme Love

which transforms the Earthly into the angel of one's house, the soul into the Spouse of Christ, and the body into the Temple that

> . . . keeps its shrine
> Sacred to Heaven.

With her religious charm, candor, and simplicity, her high faith, deep emotion, beautiful austerity, her theme of renouncement, and the splendor of perfection, Alice Meynell is the "Lady Abbess of the Nineties." The summation of her relation with the infinite is, to use her own words, "Heavily on this little heart Presses this immortality." In view of this immortality, she so celebrates her dominant mood of renouncement, that she might have walked the Umbrian Hills with the Little Poor Man.

But in Francis Thompson one ascends the heights of mysticism, that state of longing for the personal embrace of Infinity. In that suspension from the consciousness of time, Thompson attains Desire exceeding desire and unattainable. And in his poetry he not only suffers the little ones to come unto the Master, but himself becomes one of them: his purity of soul has kept his heart a child's that he may be of the Kingdom of Heaven.

From the agnosticism and pessimism of such as Arthur Hugh Clough and James Thomson, the Pre-Raphaelite Brotherhood was an escape into romanticism. Like the poets of the orthodox protest, they turned to the past for religious impulse and found it in mediaeval Italy.

If the Pre-Raphaelites did lead to Aestheticism, Pater's Epicureanism, and Henley's Stoicism, in Christina Rossetti they are immortalized as the impetus to the religious revolt at the close of the century. She is like the "Anglican Nun of the Nineteenth Century." High faith she had and she returned it to God in rhythm. On the other side of the Atlantic, Emily Dickinson, the New England Mystic, construed her belief in the Trinity into such revealed verse as:

> In the name of the bee
> And of the butterfly
> And of the breeze, amen.

The last decade of the age offered protest as did the rest of the century. The Decadents were an instance of the further escape into Romanticism. Their principle was purely a literary one: Beauty for Beauty's sake. Gathering roses while they might, they were a cult of dancing pagans. One walked alone, as a young monk among them: Lionel Johnson. He was the interpretation of "whiteness," the outstanding word of the Nineties. He witnessed poets turn from a worship of Cynara to the anointing oil of Dowson's "Extreme Unction" for a renewal of lost innocence. Symonds, Beardsley, and Blunt were happy in conversion. And each wrote a "De Profundis" in poetry, the language of the heart. What they saw poetry do is what history often does: repeat itself. Thus the nineteenth century closed in protest and conversion. In its end was its own beginning. And there was another beginning, placed on the threshold of this contemporary age. It faced both ways: back to the spiritual conflicts of the Victorian Era and forward to more than a quarter of a century that still has Merediths, Arnolds, Tennysons, and Rossettis.

> *In shadows deeper than engulfing night*
> *These radiant blossoms of the soul were bred,—*
> *They spring from victories steadfast faith has won.*
>
> PRAYER by Thomas S. Jones, Jr.

BOOK ONE: LOVERS OF EARTHLY BEAUTY

JOHN HALL WHEELOCK:

A doubting intellect and a believing heart

LETTER FROM JOHN HALL WHEELOCK

I am naturally very happy to learn that you are going to touch upon my poetry in your thesis, and more than eager to be of any help within my power.

I am not sure that I fully understand your question but I shall try to answer it according to my understanding of it. As regards the Unknown, my intellectual reactions are those suitable to the meaning implicit in the word— that is to say, humble ignorance and reverent agnosticism. This covers the domain of the intellect, which is, however, only a small part of us. Where my feelings are concerned, I have perhaps a rather blind faith, but I am unable to formulate it. I can only indicate it, as I have done many times in my poems. If you care to consult my book, "The Bright Doom," and will read there the longish poem entitled "Affirmation," you will get the gist of my position.

September 7, 1933.

ONE

STOPFORD BROOKE, speaking of the weariness of
agnosticism in the literature of the mid-nineteenth
century, said:

> The waves of that disturbance are still, with diminished
> force, breaking on the shores of society.

The thirty-five years that have intervened since that obser-
vation have continued to feel the dispiritedness in literature arising from the religious negation of those who
question man's capability to "know the reality correspond-
ing to his ultimate, scientific, philosophic, and religious
ideas." Among the representative poets who assume this
conscious attitude of doubt, denial, or disbelief towards
some of man's powers of knowing is John Hall Wheelock.
Confessedly, he is agnostic. In a personal communication
he has written the following:

> As regards the Unknown, my intellectual reactions are
> those suitable to the meaning implicit in the word—that
> is to say humble ignorance and reverent agnosticism.

Although he professes an agnostic intellect, he combines
with it a believing heart, for he adds:

> Where my feelings are concerned, I have perhaps a rather
> blind faith, but I am unable to formulate it. I can only
> indicate it, as I have done many times in my poems. If you
> care to consult my book *The Bright Doom* and read there
> the longish poem entitled *Affirmation*, you will get the
> gist of my position.

A study of the poetry of John Hall Wheelock brings
home to one a sense of everlasting doubt pursued by a
heart desirous of belief. Throughout the three volumes,

5

Dust and Light, The Black Panther, and *The Bright Doom*, which for their agnostic consciousness are more significant than the earlier volumes, there is the sense of religious unrest. The soul of the poet is oppressed with the thought of mortality; peace will come only when he is at home in death in the arms of Earth, his beautiful one. The verses are impregnated with the weariness of an ever-inquiring mind trying to explore vast immensity and to fill inconsolable vacancy and eternal voids. They are the nostalgia of a soul breaking down the barriers of tragic gloom for an escape from the inexorable silence and the passion of pain and regret, born and reborn perpetually, in a troubled heart.

Placed at the end of his last publication, the poem, "Affirmation" is the *Summa* of John Hall Wheelock. It is the exposition of his creed. It brings us face to face with a realization of "the humble ignorance and the reverent agnosticism" that he confesses and the believing heart that he intimates. But the following lines seem especially to indicate the temper of his soul:

> Wondering; doubting; grieving; worshipping—
> Perplexed before the mystery of things.

The essence of the poem, they are the essence of his contribution to literature. They are the key not only to "Affirmation," which is the final expression of his attitude, but to most of his other work. The two lines lie occult in his very titles: *Dim Wisdoms, The Bright Doom, Tumult, The Lost Traveller's Dream, Space and Solitude, Dust and Light,* and *The Black Panther*. The title of this poem which is the summation of his beliefs is in accordance with the incongruity of the tenets of agnosticism: that we can know nothing with certainty. The term "Affirmation" is, then, like the principle itself, self-refuting; for if we cannot know anything with certainty, neither can the assertion be known. Therein the poet is consistently agnostic.

"Affirmation" holds Mr. Wheelock's belief in the unity of life. He seems to contend that there is one vitalizing force that invigorates all being, partakes of the individuality of each through the ages, and sheds its generations like dead leaves. He calls this unifying principle: "One Self—the spirit of Man; for we are one." Thus all men are one in attitude: they are in communion with one another in plight, in doom (which word is an earmark of the poet), in stubborn questioning, in the sympathetic understanding of their insecurity in life, in the insatiable thirst for knowledge of what may be, and in their challenging curiosity over the atom and the cell. Men are united in deed as well. Their limitations are universal whether they are in the space of iron cities or the solitude of country life. Their restlessness moves in unchanging divers ways: they brood apart, but laugh with the multitude; they conquer the soil, build up towards heaven, wander the ocean wastes, and witness the tragedy of Man proceed from birth to death.

> We grapple with each other; we hate; we fear; we kill;
> We cry aloud; we yearn, kneeling in prayer,
> Lifting our faces to the emptiness.

In the procession of the dead, men found their own selves. To them life held out the same desires and appetites. They wondered, "Asked the old questions—and, like us, in vain"; and now they rest as they did in preexistence.

To the poet, however, the Voice that will summon all to the same refuge is a lonely and an inevitable one. There

is no sense of returning home to the Father, but rather
to the dust, to be blown to the four distant corners of
the world. With heavy plaint, he asks: "Is there no respite
from the wheel of things?" But he knows that all existence
moves

> In iron bondage, to the eternal Rhythm,
> Whose meaning and whose end we may not guess;

and that the prayer of agnostic thought will never pierce
the clouds. To restless minds he says:

> Yet be assured that all is well
> And the truth greater than we dare to dream—
> Greater and more exalted! Though the mind,
> Fashioned for humbler uses, may not grasp
> The meaning of the mystery.

His believing heart discovers that there is in each a self
that weathers all the storms of chance with a belief that
cannot be stifled, and that the growing things of earth
proclaim idealism:

> And every heart-beat is an act of faith,
> Praising the hidden Purpose.

But the intellect prevails and the poet is back to reality.
These realities, he reassures us, are grim and austere. In
the same fatalistic and agnostic strain, he continues:

> . . . the wheel of heaven
> Revolves, with all its motions, and the planet
> Heaves forward blindly, bearing us along
> Into the Void—we know not why nor where.

But Mr. Wheelock is not defeated spiritually, for that
controlling spirit which all through his poetry he calls
"One Self," which has lived in the past and will survive
to the end, inspires to courage and faith. Consistently, we

ask: courage to do what? and faith to believe what? But the poet in three supplementary sonnets determines faith as the gauge of life. Mind and heart labor toward the Unknown, but in the final solution of the riddle of eternity the heart

> Jetting fierce streams of faith—with every beat,
> In sacramental affirmation, pours
> Life's answer through the unbelieving brain.

Perhaps the best instance of the poet's reaction to the demands of agnosticism is his tribute to the Mind. He knows its propensities, its infinite patience in driving out hope from within and without. And then in thoroughly sympathetic understanding, he addresses the Mind as "Your own best lover and your own worst friend." A disease of the mind can be remedied only by the mind, says Chesterton. But just now Mr. Wheelock's cannot effect the cure. Throughout his last three books, his mind has been in a condition of stasis. There has been no spiritual evolution within the scope of the publications, for in one of his earlier poems, he assumes the position which he maintains in his later poems:

> Let me, baffled still, yet still believing,
> In the darkness loyal to the light,
> Deep within this exiled bosom bear it
> Silent, the great faith forevermore.[1]

In these verses we note the same key of

> Wondering; doubting; grieving; worshipping—
> Perplexed before the mystery of things,

that is the "Open Sesame!" to "Affirmation" and to the belief of the poet.

Wonder, doubt, doom, and an undefined faith are the

motifs that he uses in his poetry. There is excessive repetition of the words: "baffled," "bewilderment," "inflexible,"
"inexorable," "doom," "inevitable," "hopeless," "oblivion"
and "blind." All are agnostic earmarks.

Mr. Wheelock seems to have little escape from wonder.
Frequently he writes:

> Ah, I cannot understand![2]
> How shall I understand these things?[3]

All day he is confronted with the sense of the "ancient
Awe," the "inmost Awe," and at night when he reads,
he says:

> And yet, even in loveliness I find
> No refuge from old wonder; the old thoughts
> And the old questions come to mind.[4]

The questions are all of the tenor of agnosticism, the
queries of a mind trying to probe the First Cause and resting in the hopelessness of a mind that will ever be un-
persuaded:

> Alas, what has your dreaming brought you to![5]
> Are you content! How is it with you now?[6]

Such are his thoughts when he thinks of Ernest Dowson
and Tchaikovsky. At night in his dreams he hears music
which opens up to him worlds which he is incapable of
knowing now. His human mind can only wonder where
it is the harper sits playing

> Over and over, with such high and dreadful peace,
> The passion and sorrow of the eternal doom?[7]

Beethoven's symphonies still the warring voices of his soul
when, again, he visions in their sound endless vistas. He
says that his spirit leaves his face, "O hungering face
turned on an empty goal." Life seems like music to him

with its "alternations of the grave and the glad," but ending with the sad. Feeling everything, but being unable with his agnostic mind to comprehend, he runs the race of life, laughing and weeping, with the darkness blinking his vision.

Even footsteps excite his wonder. He sees man and beast following the same road to the same end.

> What country is it that they all are seeking,
> Who up and down the world, by night or day,
> Move with such patience, always to one end?[8]

The sea moves him likewise. But as in other instances, it leaves his vision blurred and renews his old hopes, but all in vain. As he looks upon the eternal vacancies extending "far as the wandering wings of thought may grope," he is wholly dispirited and asks

> To what dark purpose was the Will employed
> That fashioned, ere the dawn of Time grew dim,
> The waste of ocean.[9]

With the same hopelessness, he begs a message from the Will that wrought it and the firmament.

To assuage his sense of wonder, twice he dallies with false surmise. The first event is in "The Divine Fantasy" when, in a mode similar to that of Rossetti's "Blessed Damosel," a brother from across the darkness questions, assures, and reassures the poet in his belief. It is the belief that he has outlined in the key poem "Affirmation": the principle of the One Self:

> . . . the fierce carnival
> Of death and passion, wherein each and all
> Mix, and are mingled, slaughter, blend, and pass
> Each into other—the high poem that has
> No end and no beginning, that the one

> Self in all living forms beneath the sun,
> And in all worlds around him and above,
> Weaves on the strands of hunger, death, and love.

The experience leaves him encouraged in his agnosticism, and, as a faithful disciple of the Dread Loveliness, he implores it to be strong in him that all his verse may be the expression of "its groping utterance, across the intangible abyss of thought."

"Toward the Bright Doom" is the other of his false surmises. It marks the climax of his wonder. Like his "Divine Fantasy," it suggests an influence. It seems to revert to Newman's "Dream of Gerontius." But it is the dream of an agnostic soul rebelling against its limitations as it struggles to reach the ancient goal toward which everything gropes its way. The soul perceives the narrow confines of his room become transformed into immensity; it finds itself on the margin of death's kingdom.

> Tiptoe my spirit trembled and elate
> With expectation of far things to be.

All the anguish of life has passed; he feels relieved of the weight of mortality as he is borne by a visible Presence away from earth. Despite the assurance of the Presence that he can never escape from passion, pain, and death, and that Christ is still a victim

> For the old doom, from age to age
> Making His Everlasting pilgrimage
> In lonely splendor down the starry way;

the soul persists in seeking the abode of God. But all his desire is met with futile hope:

> Though from heaven's deeps to heaven's heights above
> You see him, though through all eternity
> You send your soul out in one loneliest cry,

No voice shall answer, nor no tongue declare
The Presence that is all things everywhere—
The flying Dream.

But the spirits pass on in flight until they reach mid-heaven, where a voice offers a draught, Oblivion, to the soul that he may drink and merge his own self with the self of all that live and thus attain to immortality. But his reluctance to do so, elicits from the voice the sentence of the tragic destiny and the triumphant doom which no life can escape. All nature, all loveliness,

> Moves without murmur, and accepts the doom—
> Yea, even this, the most beloved too!
> Now in this thought perish the thought of you,
> And in the wonder and the dream thereof
> Cease and be one at last with all you love.

The counsel of the voice to take refuge from wonder in oblivion serves the poet in other instances. Very often we find him apostrophizing Nirvana

> Deep I drink of you, divine
> Dizzy draught, bewildering wine;[10]
> . . . and we drank,
> Dizzy with dread joy and sacrificial
> Rapture of self-loss and sorrow dear,
> Deep of Beauty's draught, divine Nirvana,
> The bewildering wine of all the world;[11]
> Deeper and deeper let me drink and draw—
> Nirvana, divine oblivion.[12]

Annihilation or absorption into the divine would give him beatific freedom from the obsession of doubt as well. Throughout the three volumes already referred to, Mr. Wheelock wanders, as did Arnold and Clough, between two worlds. To him nature itself partakes of his attitude of perplexity. As he walks in autumn along the beach, the waters "Are doubtful, half in hope, and half in fear." Over the sea there are alternations of light and shadow. Far out on the void, he sees a lone bird tossed about on the floor of the sea. In the flight of the bird through almost endless space, he finds kinship: its veering motion is the faltering of his own spirit's amid the buffetings of doubt.

> Far though she fare, far though her flight aspire—
> However far—it shall be but to find
> New wastes beyond, new ways for the desire
> Of the unfathomable and spacious Mind.
>
> In the vast reaches of His meditation—
> The sorrowful distances—her stricken wings
> Flag, failing her; my heart's imagination
> Faints, in the lonely endlessness of things.[13]

Night with its fears aggravates his doubt. All the circumstances of darkness: owls, moths, the ticking of a clock, the gnawing of a mouse, old phantoms, a distant echo, and the wail of sorrow renew "the ancient doubt." As he thinks at night of the heroes of the world that now are in everlasting silence,

> Pondering these,
> The fretful spirit in bewilderment
> Quickens with a vague doubt, and not content,
> Broods—and is ill at ease.[14]

The beauty of the heavens raises eternal bewilderment.

> So shall it be!
> Till heaven yield her sceptre; till the throne
> Of night be shaken, and the Face be known
> Beyond eternity.[15]

Here on earth man cannot hope to realize as his highest hope anything beyond man is the poet's sad belief.

All men, he says, in the spirit of agnosticism, are wanderers. They "roam and range the hills of chance . . ." and comfort one another through the communion of speech. Despite death, doubt, and doom, they have within them the old ecstasy of hearing.

> Praise of the road, doubt for the journey's end
> Or of the purpose of the pilgrimage,
> (If there *be* purpose in the pilgrimage)
> Questions, questions and reassurances.[16]

They are one also in the blind struggle of life. "Baffled and faint, incredulous and dumb," they have no trust in the merits of the conflict which they wage before the tide of the battle turns unfavorably for them, or as the poet says:

> . . . and it has been so
> From the beginning and, for all we know
> It shall be, to that end none may discern.[17]

Perplexed always before the Ancient Awe, men can never know wisdom. The poets have, perhaps, "dim wisdoms," but, for men in general, wisdom is still unborn:

> Wisdom, the ghost of beauty, in the wide
> Womb of the world lies clamoring for life,
> While the white Beauty, the immortal Bride,
> Sits throned upon the summits void of strife.[18]

All the wisdom of the sages and the beauty of the poet's inspiration is not to be compared with a flower springing from the ground or with Helen's beauty. Man is incapable of knowing. He can only doubt and wonder about "that land beyond that they have never found."

What fiery one here set
His throne in splendor?[19]

Where may I moor my bark?[20]

. . . Can it be,
The form from which this thrilling passion flows
. . . relapsed
Into the formless?[21]

These and many others are the questions that reveal
the doubting spirit of the poet. But more significant of his
perplexity is "The Black Panther." The title suggests the
pent-up feelings of Mr. Wheelock in his gropings for
certainty. Doubt is the panther which moves back and
forth in silent rage within the breast of the poet. In steady
and relentless quest, it tries the walls of its prison. The
poet says:

All day I feed him with my living heart;
    But when the night puts forth her dreams and stars,
    The inexorable Frenzy reawakes:
His wrath is hurled upon the trembling bars,
    The eternal passion stretches me apart,
And I lie silent—but my body shakes.

The "Lion House" closes the volume of *The Black Panther*
as the title poem opens it. It finds Mr. Wheelock still in
doubt.

As through a haunted brain—
    With tireless footfalls
The Obsession moves again,
    Trying the floor, the walls,
Forever, but in vain.

And in the sonnet "Zenith," the one self within the poet
stands in perfect fulfillment and wars on the "dark foe":
doubt.

We have met the poet in his wonders, doubts, perplexities. He adds in the quotation that he "worships." In his verses, he does pay homage to the Deity under different forms. Never, however, is there the adoration given to a personal God. In the three volumes is prevalent the idea of the One Being who is all and in whom all are One. It is the "Will of this being that all creatures serve in darkness to their woven doom." Men and animals, the good and the evil are all "Blind Players" taking part in the one-patterned drama of life as the Great Will has planned it. But their conflicts are, likewise, those of the One of which they are a part. Rest will come only when the Inexorable is placated by their offering, which will always be the offering of violence. All tumult is due to the One Will exercising its love, pity, and joy among the blindly warring many. These attitudes both approach fatalism, as does

> My dreams wear thinner as the years go by:
>> The stony face of Fate into my own
> Stares with that granite look of hers; and I
>> Stare back, with a still face—but not of stone.[22]

Vaguely he calls God, Love. But it is not the love of Christian Charity.

When the poet worships, it is generally the Unknown that he addresses. Sometimes he does call upon God specifically, but the appellation is no more than a symbol of the feeling of the human heart for the Great Unknowable of the Intellect. With the title of "Father," he eulogizes the sun. "Sundown" is a little "Te Deum" chanted to "our Father, the sun." In another poem he begs from it a benediction: "Hallow me, my father—even me." Are not these in the precincts of Pantheism?

But to the earth and to dust he pays supreme tribute. We are all part of the earth, having been made of her dust. But the poet does not recognize the fact that this dust is animated with a soul that has come from God. Earth lends her substance to us, and, as we are interred, she reclaims it. Mr. Wheelock would have us believe from "Earth" that in the dust along with Plato's brain there is the heart of Christ. Wheelock deifies the dust. It is "God asleep." Again, he says,

> Here in the hollow of my hand
> A bit of God Himself I keep,
> Between two vigils fallen asleep.[23]

The poet does render homage with perhaps a blind faith, as he says, but his worship is that of the god of agnosticism, remote and undefined. Yet in his key poem, "Affirmation," he does take exception and makes the act of faith of a sceptic:

> . . . And as for Him
> Whom we have sought beyond the stars in vain,
> Perhaps He may be nearer than we know.

Yet here again the poet's desire to believe is crowded with the doubting word "perhaps." But his believing heart which he confesses and which speaks in his poetry, excludes him from the recent agnostics who deny as well as doubt. His is not the combination of agnosticism and atheism so prevalent today. If we may trace the reason for his attitude of belief, perhaps we may find it in his own lines addressed to Tolstoi:

> Look on this face, and ponder on him well
> Who was the first to cleave the unknown seas!—
> Upon this brow broke the new thought of the world
> Whose waves we wander now with furrowing keel.

Edna St. Vincent Millay

Revels in her love of earth

TWO

WHEN Elinor Wylie, shortly before her death, wrote in a "Letter to V——," whom we know to be Edna St. Vincent Millay,

> No, V——, you will never persuade me
> That Death is other than a friend;
> I can't believe the hand that made me
> Shall so unmake me in the end,

she refuted the chief tenet of Miss Millay's belief:

> Greater am I
> By the earth's girth
> Than Mighty Death!
> All creatures cry
> That can summon breath
> And speak no lie.
>
> For he is nothing;
> He is less
> Than Echo answering
> Nothingness.[1]

Edna St. Vincent Millay is an egocentric lyrist: she suffuses her poetry with herself. But

> Great poetry is concerned with the deepest feelings of the individual and the greatest issues of life, with high aspirations and spiritual experiences.[2]

Hence Miss Millay takes account of poetry as the persistent cry of the soul and introduces into it a spirituality, essential and clear. But the spirituality is neither ascetic nor pious. It is rather the force of her exquisitely sensitive soul impelling whether for good or evil.

Surveying the poetry of Edna St. Vincent Millay to discover her consciousness of a Supreme Being, one finds her assuming the attitude of pantheism and paganism. Throughout her work there is advance, but her belief never rises from the slough of pagan despond. Early in her poetic life, she was an adherent of a seeming pantheism; later she acquired more definite views on life, love, and death. At times she seemed stoic; yet, despite what passed for belief, she was merely attitudinizing. Her latest poetry sounds the depths of her convictions: despair, the tragedy of life and living, the bitterness of beauty, the cruelty of love, and the mockery of death.

"Renascence," the title poem of her first publication, offers beauty as the solution of the tragedy of life. By losing herself in its cult, she will be wholly detached from self. She will be so absorbed by cosmic beauty that all sorrow will be dispersed. At nineteen she could write:

> The soul can split the sky in two,
> And let the face of God shine through.

In her ecstasy of spirit, the radiant identity of God will never escape her. If He moves across the grass, her eyes will be quick to see Him; and, if He speaks, however silently, she will answer Him. In "God's World," her canticle to the universe, she rises to the heights of nature mysticism. With the same fervor and the degree of intense passion with which a mystic in the spiritual order longs for the personal embrace of God, she craves the contact of the cosmos:

> . . . That gaunt crag
> To crush! To lift the lean of that black bluff!
> World, world, I cannot get thee close enough!

To her the natural is all-sufficient. All beauty, she says, stretches her apart: whether it be the mist, the moonlight, or human charm. She has become so inured to it that she is nourished by its excess.

But apart from this attitude of pagan abandon, note a quality of renunciation. She says that she will look at the skies, the rocks, the clouds with "quiet eyes." She will, likewise, watch the grass bend and rise by the wind. And then she adds,

> I will touch a hundred flowers
> And not pick one.[3]

In her first volume she manifests no understanding of her relation to life. She asks often, "What is my life to me?" Consequently, her ideas of death are equally undefined. When she lyricizes a friend in death, she is perplexed concerning his state of existence. Does heaven hold him? Has he become a part of earth again?

Theoretically and practically, she is an unbeliever inasmuch as she expresses the wish to feel the faith that temporizes grief. She recognizes the value of faith, but the Faith she would prize seems to control even God.

In her succeeding volumes, *A Few Figs from Thistles, Second April,* and *The Harp Weaver,* her views are still static. She has no philosophy of life to establish sound doctrine for herself on the elemental truths of existence. To her at this period, life is nothing but "An empty cup, a flight of uncarpeted stairs." Love is no more "Than the great tide that treads the shifting shore." But she remains firm in her allegiance to nature worship: beauty is still her god. Nor does indisposition, mental or physical, of any kind interfere with the practice of her devotion.

Death, at this period, is merely a destroyer. To be consistently pagan, Miss Millay not only assumes the attitude of the cult, but she returns to the period itself for medita-

tion. When she considers the victims of death, she notes
that

> Lesbia with her sparrow
> Shares the darkness.[4]

When a friend dies, she prays to Persephone to be maternal
to the little one in Hell and to console her with

> . . . My dear, my dear,
> It is not so dreadful here.[5]

And in that same pagan aura, she looks for Silence.
With the same spiritual ardor of the "Hound of Heaven,"
she seeks Silence down "that dolorous labyrinth" where
light never reaches. She seeks her among the upper gods,
but to no purpose. Finally Euterpe assures her that Silence
is found only in Oblivion. But that abode Edna St. Vincent
Millay can reach through her adoration of nature. She will
partake of the draught "savoring faintly of the acid earth."
Pagan, too, are the antecedents of her word of honor and
her spirit of love: she swears with the heart of Lilith; she
loves with the love of Lesbia and Lucrece. In her love
ceremonial there is no reverence, for it celebrates the deed
of Isolde and of Guinevere. Instead of the usual libation
offered at Love's Feast, she tells us, in a sonnet sequence,
that the Lovers drenched the altars with shouts and
laughter. They bound their sacrilegious brows with the
sacred myrtle, and made sport with the holy grove. Love
was so offended that, although they should offer their
bodies to the flame, it could never be propitiated, for

> . . . here
> Henceforward is a grove without a name,
> A pasture to the shaggy goats of Pan,
> Whence flee forever a woman and a man.[6]

"The Curse" is anticipatory of a later attitude toward death. Paganism does not admit the idea of immortality. Death, it holds, is the be-all and the end-all of existence here. Miss Millay, therefore, imagines her ashes being blown across the sea as a fish scale or a butterfly wing. Various are the forms one's dust assumes, she holds. Sometimes it "will settle at the root that climbs about your door."

In "The Feast" Miss Millay falls into the attitudinizing of one bordering on stoicism. To her there is no wine nor fruit as wonderful as thirst or want. She says:

> Feed the grape and bean
> To the vintner and monger;
> I will lie down lean
> With my thirst and my hunger.

Again she seems to be posing here:

> I see so clearly how my life must run
> One year behind another year until
> At length these bones that leap into the sun
> Are lowered into the grave, and lie still,
> I would at times the funeral were done,
> And I abandoned on the ultimate hill.[7]

In *The Buck in the Snow,* she threw herself completely into the idea that love is a fallacious thing, that death is inexorable, that beauty is disillusioning, cruel, and impossible; and that life is only a foredoom. Yet, in these notes of despair, there is still spirituality in the sense understood by Edna St. Vincent Millay. She suffers keenly in her exquisite soul as she travels her hopeless way. Of her sensitivity to suffering, she makes note often, as in "Mist in the Valley." Hurt to the breaking point, she says that the hills hurt her yet more.

But in the midst of her despair, she can send out challenges in song of rebellion, insubordination, and irreconciliation with the realities of life. "Moriturus" might be taken as her key poem in these respects. While she challenges Death, she idealizes it. As "insensate matter," she wishes to be interred in the grave, but to be treated as "sensate me." That circumstance is impossible. But it is the poet's way of posing to avoid the terror of soul. Granted the condition, however, Miss Millay will enjoy the grave and daringly defy Death who is, according to her belief, no more than a "spongy wall," a "sticky river," a "Thief," "The Maggot in the Cheese," "The Canker in the Leaf." Her fight with Death will endure until Life is gone. Meanwhile, she boasts defiantly of her part in the combat. But since Death is inevitable and immortality not within the prospect of her belief, she can only despair as

> With his hand on my mouth
> He shall drag me forth,
> Shrieking to the south
> And clutching at the north.[8]

Nowhere has she any expression of Christian resignation, for death, being the end of existence, makes both the lovers and the thinkers one with the indiscriminate dust. She says that "the best is lost, I know. But I do not approve. And I am not resigned." And in "Hangman's Oak," she makes similar moan:

> Side by side together in the belly of Death
> We sit without hope.

The same "unmitigated dark" is in "To the Wife of a Sick Friend."

Whereas Miss Millay in her early work was "waylaid by beauty," now she faces the truth in a dark manner. And as is philosophically correct, it is not beauty to her. She finds herself overwhelmed with anguish and thus she cries out in her distraction:

> I would to God I were quenched and fed
> As in my youth
> From the flask of song, and the good bread
> Of beauty richer than truth.[9]

For comfort she would turn to the river Lethe, where as a fervid disciple she could drink of its waters, waters that relieve pain and restore beauty, that beauty "richer than truth." She goes back to the same pagan aura in her poem "To Jesus on His Birthday," for she recognizes no Divinity in Him. She feels that the gospels are less than the wind and that Christmas means only a yard of tinsel and the other decorations that make it a commercial festival. Christ's birth and death are lost upon the world for

> The stone the angel rolled away with tears
> Is back upon your mouth these thousand years.[10]

This sonnet, written perhaps in criticism, is her only allusion to the source of Christian Love, for everything else is pure paganism.

It is in accord with the fundamental theme of *The Buck in the Snow* that she closes the book with her reaction "On Hearing a Symphony of Beethoven." Music, alone, is excellent and peaceful. A moment of music is the best the world can offer amid its many tragedies and occasions for despair. But that is the pagan view. Life holds comfort with its tragedies. It is the mission of Christianity to shatter the gloom of paganism. But when Miss Millay reverts to a pagan civilization, music must be the only "Tranquil blossom on the tortured stem."

In "Fatal Interview," the poet's pagan attitude is at the

point of crystallization. In fifty-two sonnets, she writes a treatise on unrequited love. It is the autobiography of a soul that never saw beyond the natural. Were the motive of her love supernaturalized or even preternaturalized, the treatise would be a study in Catholic mysticism. But the poet misses God by a hair's breadth; that small margin, however, is the difference between paganism and Christianity. From a consideration of her attitude toward beauty in her first volume *Renascence*, it was inevitable that some fatal interview would come into her life. So universal was her early love that the human fails now to satiate her longing. In her scheme of love, there is deep spirituality; she gives herself completely. That is entirely God-like, but her intention is at the opposite pole of Christian Love. There is no loving for God's sake.

> I think however that of all alive
> I only in such utter, ancient way
> Do suffer love.[11]

Hers is the love of Dido for Aeneas.

In each of the sonnets in the series, the poet gives a different aspect of love. She has experienced each. Here again in the series, she enjoys the pagan mood; and so she returns to the pagan civilization. She invokes the Olympian gods, monsters of vice and crime, and tells them that her son will be "Branded with godhead, heel and brow and thigh," being half-human, half-divine, as are all the heroes of pagan myths. And loyal, in her paganism, she pledges fealty to Venus, the "Sparrow Drawn" and to Cupid, her "arrowy child." She dreams, too, of pagan culture. She moves among the Elysian fields with Europa, Danae, Leda, all mortal women, "who had a god for guest."

Yet there are instances of her investing pagan times with Christian attitudes, for Edna St. Vincent Millay can bring a tearful sorrow when she says:

> Since of no creature living the last breath
> Is twice required, or twice the ultimate pain,
> Seeing how to quit your arms is very death,
>   'Tis likely that I shall not die again.[12]

She is Christian also when she counsels against beauty as the sole criterion for marriage.

Sonnet XXXIX marks the climax of her love when she bids the god depart. Then with a cry, far from paganism, she pays this beautiful tribute to Christian marriage: "Two with a light who match their steps and sing."

As the sequence approaches the end, we find her having given all. All giving creates a wound. Faith is the link between knowledge and love. But Miss Millay has no faith. She will, therefore, always bear the scar of her encounter. The last sonnet is in perfect relation to those which have preceded. It is the old legend of Endymion and Diana which has juxtaposition in the love affair of the poet. The circumstances are the same:

> Whereof she wanders mad, and being all unfit
> For mortal love, that might not die of it.[13]

Again she has given her message to the world. And it is paganism.

Miss Millay would dispense with the belief in future happiness with God for all eternity. She has no use for a state dependent upon our personal relations with the Being Who will judge us according to our love. She herself has an infinite capacity for loving, but paganism caters to mortality only. Yet, humanity will never fill the goblet of her desire. So she must yearn always. There is one way open to her: pagan stoicism. But she can never reach stoicism, for her loving heart will never permit that indifference. With her vigorous intensity, she will go on in the spirit of paganism as when she says:

> Heart, have no pity on this house of bone:
> Shake it with dancing, break it down with joy.
> No man holds mortgage on it; it is your own;
> To give, to sell at auction, to destroy.
>
> All that delightful youth forbears to spend
> Molestful age inherits, and the ground
> Will have us; therefore while we're young, my friend—
> The Latin's vulgar, but the advice is sound.[14]

The advice is pagan also, but in her belief there is no merit because she can write of death thus:

> For he is nothing;
> He is less
> Than Echo answering
> Nothingness.[15]

Elinor Wylie:

Toward the Light

Extracts from

SECOND LETTER FROM WILLIAM ROSE BENÉT

You are right about Elinor's "Letter to V——" being addressed to Vincent Millay. They were devoted friends, but on certain things did not see eye to eye. I shall never forget, however, certain days at "Steepletop," where Miss Millay and her husband Eugen Boissevain live, when we visited them, and both Elinor and Vincent reading their poems to each other. Neither shall I ever forget that after Elinor's death, when Vincent was first apprised of the fact and was reading that night in Brooklyn, she put aside the reading her own work and read entirely from Elinor's. The poetic sympathy between them was genuine and lasting. So far as the question of immortality was concerned, and on the religious side—they differed at times. Elinor had no conventional religion though she had been brought up an Episcopalian. Both the sermons and the poetry of John Donne had, however, a strong effect upon her. I think she never lost a certain modicum of childlike faith, though even I am hardly credentialled to speak of her in that regard. She was God's own child, anyway!

August 4, 1934

WILLIAM ROSE BENÉT 502 W. 12 St.,
NEW YORK CITY

Dear Sister Mary Dowd:

Elinor Wylie, born Elinor Morton Hoyt, was brought up as an Episcopalian. As agnostic in later years she still retained religious feeling in the truest & deepest sense though — unmistakenly of no church. As you in the death she had evinced leaning in the poetry & prose of John Donne. As a poem found posthumously, as I mark the comment, she expressed her religious:

And recite this list call this Majesty, God, & Elizabeth & Jude, "Verger Vital" And so deep in earth, "Rosa Mira" upon the dead.

They printed my letter there, which bore on this other matter, & if you can procure from them a copy of the issue on Trinity it particulary is in her best book, "Angels & Earthly Creatures" the whose spiritual element is the best, is apparent. She found with a white flame.

Very sincerely yours,
William Rose Benét

New York,
February 23,
1931.

THREE

A STUDY of Elinor Wylie's poetry logically follows one on Edna St. Vincent Millay's religious attitude; they were friends and rivals. When we stated before that in a "Letter to V——" Elinor Wylie refuted a tenet of Miss Millay's belief, we definitely established one of her own views on religion. Of that view, the last stanza of the poem is especially revealing:

> And, while I live, I'll call Him MIGHTY,
> Yes, and ELOQUENT and JUST;
> And scratch in earth: INTEGER VITAE;
> And: DOLCE MORS upon the dust.

These lines mark one of the differences between the religious beliefs of Edna St. Vincent Millay and Elinor Wylie: the question of immortality. Whereas Edna St. Vincent Millay calls death "a maggot," "nothing," Elinor Wylie declares:

> Although they burn me on a faggot
> I turn me to my Father's house;
> I will not have Him called a Maggot;
> I will not have Him called a Louse.[1]

In a letter to the author of this study, her husband, William Rose Benét, corroborates the inference:

> You are right about Elinor's "Letter to V——" being addressed to Vincent Millay. They were devoted friends, but on certain things did not see eye to eye. So far as the question of immortality was concerned, and on the religious side—they differed at times.

On a previous occasion he wrote:

> An agnostic in late years she still retained religious feeling

in the truest and deepest sense though a member of no church.

And he wrote in *The Commonweal*:

> She worshipped courage. She herself had suffered deeply, and still suffered proudly from early recklessness. How great her own courage was, how strong her intellectual integrity, it is my privilege to have known.

It is to this last tribute that some of the poetry of Elinor Wylie seems to bear accurate witness, for it preaches stoicism. Here is another distinction between the credo of Edna St. Vincent Millay and that of Miss Wylie. Whereas the former needs stoicism for serenity of spirit, the latter attained its perfection. Unlike Miss Millay, Elinor Wylie shows no spiritual drive in her verse. Hers is no power impelling her spirit to heights from which the merely human must recoil, but, instead, her soul is adamant to all happening about her. Hence, what she has written is poetry born of cold flame, echoing a soul unbowed by joy or grief, but freely submissive to natural laws of things. Her style is, therefore, Grecian in thought and in emotion, and her diction is correspondingly reflective of her attitude. Is there undue repetition of words like "cold," "stones," "gray," "monotones," "dead," "scorn," and "inscrutable"? Yet from the austerity of her mood they are consistent. With the same sense of fitness, she sets the dominant temper of that mood when she says with Shelley: "Desolation is a delicate thing."

Truly a stoic, Elinor Wylie passes through sorrow unafraid; sorrow which was to take heavy toll becomes wholly elusive. Sorrow more apparently burdensome than clay on the grave in winter she found as short-lived as frost, smoke, a cloud, or a drop of dew. While she admits that her mind

would desire to hold fast to the sorrow, still her stoic heart
must be free from overmastering grief. In such grief she
must rise superior. "Desolation is a Delicate Thing" confirms the attitude:

> This sorrow, which I believed a gravestone over my heart,
> Is gone like a cloud; . . .
> It was not my heart; it was this poor sorrow alone which
> broke.

This, of course, is no proud boast.

In other exigencies, the poet maintains emotional bal-
ance. In a moment of deception on the part of one she
held most dear, when her impulses would be to yield to
killing grief, she is again unaffected, for

> It was the moment, not myself, was slain,
> And faith grew crescent in the mind again.[2]

Music also can be an effective medium in her state of
equipoise. The space of a Viennese Waltz can bridge for
her the chasm between time and eternity and serve the
same release from the temporal as does death that hovers
over her. So she sings:

> We are so tired, and perhaps tomorrow
> Will never come; be fugitive awhile
> From tears, and let the dancing drink your sorrow
> As it has drunk the colour from your smile.[3]

When she might have pity, she is unmoved, for there,
as in sorrow and death, stoicism has no entrance. Yet her
imagination can easily fashion this piece of lore, "The
Village Mystery," and feel her lack of pity in it:

> Now why should I, who walk alone
>
> .   .   .   .
>
> Turn, when a woman casts a stone
> At a beggar in a shroud.

Even in the personal experience of disloyalty she does not despair. Conscious that she is one of two who are the vassals and vessels of the same Lord to whom she has sworn not only her fidelity but her devotion to the interests of her rival as well, she can say with a brave heart and high head:

> O, if from different cups you drank a curse,
> Though yours was gold, and hers was something worse,
> I were indeed undone! But you have blessed
> Your own particular drop, and damn the rest!
>
> .   .   .   .   .
>
> The cup is loving, having kissed you once.[4]

In the contemplation and presence of death, a stoic is engrossing to study. He feels no need for sympathy. Elinor Wylie reflects her traditional stoical attitude in the following lines selected from a poem called "Speed the Parting":

> You must die—but of course you must—
> And better later than sooner.
>
> .   .   .   .   .
>
> Therefore die when you please;
> It's not very wise to worry;
> I shall not shiver and freeze;
> I shall not even be sorry.

The poem is particularly pagan. Here in the prospect of death, she mentions no thought of God, no reference to creation, love, redemption, or to the nobility of man's destiny for all eternity. But, to a stoic, death holds out no promise. The soul is merely a sublimated mass which will end in dissolution. Elsewhere Elinor Wylie defends the theory, but in others she takes offense and credits the soul with immortality. In what the world deems failure, she offers no comfort, but would imply that nothing can be retrieved: what is done cannot be undone:

> Nothing is mended
> Under the sun.[5]

Of a friend who has died she thinks only in terms of dust. In justice to earth she feels bound to scatter his ashes entirely upon the air, for then snowflakes will be softer, clouds will be more cirrous, and

> Now especially, when it is winter
>
> .   .   .   .   .
>
> Who wouldn't be glad to find a splinter
> That once was you, in the frozen grass?[6]

In her own passing, she anticipates nothing beyond. Like a saint in his cell, she says she will lie bound by scented linen in the midst of an alder wood,

> The midnight will be glassy black
>   Behind the panes, with wind about
> To set his mouth against a crack
>   And blow the candle out.

That is her "Prophecy." She realizes fully that despite her persevering efforts in the struggle, she fights for nothing, for "This is the end of all." There is no thought of reunion with the spirits of the dead, for partings here are final.

She reverences, furthermore, at times, agnosticism, admits the idea of fatalism, and denies that the only reality is perceived through the senses. As she looks over the landscape, she sees no peace, but merely a core of confusion around which has been blown in the sun a bubble, the universe, that will soon vanish. There is no virtue in it, although trees stand reverent as saints upon it. Nevertheless,

> . . . here is nothing blessed
> Save this foredoomed suspension of the end;
> Faith is the blossom, but the fruit is cursed;
> Go hence, for it is useless to pretend.[7]

Her "Confession of Faith" is arresting, for it is the profession of agnosticism, a negation of faith. In that poem, she cannot reconcile her lover's being both friend and kind. To her, he is all fear, and she defends herself against his violence.

> Whose silences portend
> A bloody end
> For lover never friend.

> But in default of faith,
> In futile breath,
> I dream no ill of death.

She knows nothing with certainty as to the place of her footsteps after death. They will be lost in the frost; they will turn somewhere under the water, or over the air,

> To earth space or stellar,
> Or the garret or cellar
> Of the house next door,[8]

while her soul will flow on as a stream

> Kissing dumb faces
> And the dusty ground.[9]

In her "Address to My Soul," she is plainly the stoic and the agnostic. She bids it to be undisturbed even though the planets are at war. It must always remain securely orbed in this contracted star.

> Fear not, pathetic flame;
> Your sustenance is doubt;
> They cannot snuff you out.

For the perfectly pagan and stoical attitude which Miss Wylie maintains, one needs the brave spirit that William Rose Benét attributes to her. Her untimely death connotes a daily struggle for her, and her frequent allusions to bravery seem charged with the desire to attain courage in order to maintain stoicism. Repeatedly she has lines like these:

> He shall be my teacher
> Who cries "Be brave,"[10]
>
> .   .   .   .
> The Brave have never died.[11]

And most significantly she resolves "to send her heart to a hard school and educate it to be brave."[12]

We have inferred that Elinor Wylie reached the perfection of a pagan stoicism, struggling in life as if there were no God, no state of ecstasy hereafter, or as if God were as ridiculous as the pagan divinities. Certainly it would seem that Miss Wylie was physically constituted to be an adherent of stoicism. She says in one of her earliest poems, "Wild Peaches":

> Down to the Puritan marrow of my bones
> There's something in this richness that I hate.
> There's something in my very blood that owns
> Bare hills, cold silver on a sky of slate.

Of these stoical characteristics, she gives ample evidence in a description of her renunciation, not through Christian detachment to honor the Supreme Being or to atone for past frailty, but wholly in the interest of the loved one whom she must "for love forget." She says,

My dearest heart, . . .
I must reject you;

. . . .

I must put you from my heart, the better to please you.[13]

And when she has stripped herself of him who was her
protection against the world, she bows her head upon a
brow of granite and kisses the moss

> For cushioning a cross
> Of racking timber sharp as childbirth bed;[14]

and adds in the same poem,

> I have embraced instead
> Of love, a ponderable cloud of rain.

She uses every means to impress this attitude on herself
and to preserve it in its perfection, as when she uses the
crude simile of the work of the bricklayer to reinforce
her spirit:

> Make my marvelous wall so thick
> Dead nor living may shake its strength.[15]

She declares that her heart will be her own valentine
because, as she sings:

> Too high, too high to pluck
> My heart shall swing.
> A fruit no bee shall suck,
> No wasp shall sting;[16]

nevertheless, she grows tired of her pretence.

The years go by "In masks outrageous and austere"; she
says she has "faced out a hundred dooms," and inquires
how long she must forbear

> The ecstasy of going hence
> And still submit to wear
> The mask of this pretence.[17]

Perhaps the most poignant of her sufferings, as may be gleaned from the preceding laments, and certainly illustrative of a subtly stoical plaint is contained in a poem addressed to her hand. She calls it "ambiguous to grasp," "secret as a fish," and "sudden as an asp." It is always under her control, but within her husband's it has the "anatomy of wax." With exquisite delicacy, she tells what might have made it like the philosopher's stone: actual instead of potential motherhood,

> If I had ever borne
> Child of our mingled blood;
> Elixirs might escape;
> But now, compact as stone,
> My hand preserves a shape
> Too utterly its own.

Delving into Greek mythology has perhaps encouraged her stoical attitude. She has kept her mind Platonic, and, in so doing has become obdurate "To those sharp ecstasies the pulses give." Hence, her use of allusions like Artemis, Theocritus, and Psyche keeps her as she says, of beauty "innocent and wild."

While Elinor Wylie reveals distinctly in certain of her poems that at some time of her life she had fully embraced stoicism, evidenced by fugitive allusions to the utter finality of things, it is likewise clear that she passed through agnosticism. This she occasionally declares in verse and William Rose Benét has also admitted it. With the same certainty, we know that she came to believe in immortality. Here she confesses it in her desire of deliverance from mortal coils and pain to enjoy the happiness of the hereafter:

> Shouldering the thoughts I loathed,
> In their corrupt disguises clothed,

> Mortality I could not tear
> From my ribs, to leave them bare
> Ivory in silver air.[18]

She makes like admission in "Hospes Comesque Corporis":

> And the small soul's dissolving ghost
> Must leave a heart-shape in the dust
> Before it is inspired and lost
> In God: I hope it must.

And in a sonnet sequence, her last publication which she arranged the day of her death, she describes the home of Divinity as being above the control of the moon and above the seas. It is "The crystal steps which climb a steeper goal." In the same sequence she complains of the weariness of mortality and commends as wise those that have shunned "This miry, world, this slough of man's despond." That death was imminent to her we learn from "My flesh was but a fresh-embroidered shroud."

This almost sudden transition from the darkness of stoicism to belief in a future life has foundation, perhaps, in a trilogy of which William Rose Benét has written:

> In regard to Elinor; It seems to me the best expression of what she felt is to be found in those marvelous last poems of hers, "Hymn to Earth," "This Corruptible," and "O Virtuous Light."

She acknowledges that a madness has possessed her mind, that her eyes have been struck blind by a sudden excess of light, that where all was naturally dark but secure, there is now confusion. Strange suns, she says, are being printed upon the secrecy of her mind. She pleads that the walls of mortality be broken to make her "spirit fugitive." In the "Hymn to Earth," she bids adieu to the incomparable element, "Whence man arose, where he shall not return,"[19] and in "This Corruptible," she addresses the body in the personification of her spirit to show that it is of man the portion which will escape into enchantment or be dissolved into nothingness. It is merely the body that is lost, disintegrated,

> Endure another hour!
> "It is but for an hour," said the spirit.[20]

This assurance she repeats in her last sonnet, published posthumously. It is a prayer for protection to the God of Hosts. Here is a recognition of Divine Protection with the idea interwoven of a Puritanic God being the Avenger. In this petition she begs God to preserve her individuality in the next life, lest by any dispensation of the Divine Will she be absorbed into another nature. Accordingly she prays:

> So that no drop of the pure spirit fall
> Into the dust: defend Thy prodigal.[21]

The whole sonnet marks her a Christian. So does the choice of themes like "The Innocents" and "Peter and John."

Elinor Wylie, as her poetry discloses, evidently was naturally a stoic, but by grace a Christian. The major part of her work, published within her lifetime, is at the nadir of stoicism. Her first poem isolates her entirely from the realm of passion: in the presence of Beauty she counsels "But love her not too much, too much." Later when she implied the denial of the truth of sense perception, she was being lifted to a state of doubt. Yet that is a step from the attitude wherein she could wish for one dead this merely pagan grace:

> On your light limbs, O loveliest,
> May the dust be light![22]

Furthermore, her heart believed, for there were prompt-ings that enlivened it with a singing sound, a Voice, she wrote, that was not her own. Wherefore she was led to the light, as she confesses in "O Virtuous Light." And that light, that grace which made her a Christian, brightened her way to unqualified belief in a state of future happiness. That conviction she sings in her last song to the world: "Take home Thy prodigal child, O Lord of Hosts!"[23]

JOHN MASEFIELD:

Poet of a mercy everlasting

FOUR

IN A lecture on "Shakespeare and Spiritual Life" John Masefield stated the cardinal principles of his religious theory: man he defined as a being composed of body, mind, and imagination; the office of the poet, in the moment of his power, he held omniscient: the seer having touched energy, the well-spring of truth, is unified with Nature: he has arrived at immanency. To Shakespeare he attributed this immanency, this power of perceiving life

> as an order of intense power, revolving with immense energy about a centre or axis, like a spinning wheel. The spinning about that centre in his vision, as in truth, is the main business of it, ordained from of old from some divine source of rhythm and harmony;[1]

and he described Mercy with this imagining:

> . . . I see a great and lovely figure, beyond all sex, throned somewhere and crowned, to whom the sharp prayer might pierce.[2]

Hereinafter, this study of Mr. Masefield's poetry will endeavor to be a testimony of the fatalism, the pantheism, and the immanentism intrinsic in the foregoing assertions.

Fate, Mr. Masefield seems to think, is omnipotent: it controls the universe and directs the actions of the individual. Blindly man submits to its dictates through the course of his life and accepts the inexorableness of the end it involves. The happy and the unhappy are in co-ordination:

> Let that which is to come be as it may,
> Darkness, extinction, justice, life intense
> The flies are happy in the summer day,

47

Flies will be happy many summers hence.
Time with his antique breeds that built the Sphynx
Time with her men to come whose wings will tower,
Poured and will pour, not as the wise man thinks,
But with blind force, to each his little hour.
And when the hour has struck, comes death or change,
Which, whether good or ill, we cannot tell,
But the blind planet will wander through her range
Bearing men like us who will serve as well.[3]

Governing the beginning of life, as Masefield puts it, "When the worm Life first started from the goal," Fate has an equally distinctive function in the state of man's pre-existence. Michael, the rejected lover in "The Daffodil Fields," finds victory in the thought that

Fate is the strongest thing, though men are strong;
Out from beyond life I was sealed to you.

When a criss-cross of circumstances occasions the happy triumph in reality, he reasons

That in another life this thing had gleamed,
This meeting by the bridge.

The conduct of Fate is inevitable. It frees no one from its jurisdiction. It demands ready compliance to its decrees. Wherefore,

However much we dawdle in the sun
We have to hurry at the touch of Fate.[4]

The fates, nevertheless, are crossed at times. Man's blindness may effect a change of destiny; the spirits of the air may devise an altered doom. Yet, always, despite the machinations of the demon powers, "Fate has his way with those who mar what is decreed."

"The Daffodil Fields" is sufficient to prove fatalism as a part of John Masefield's religious attitude. The poem reeks with the doctrine, admitting illicit triangular love on the principle that fatalism urges all on to fulfill a blind necessitous law. Predestined to share the sin of his father, to despair, and to vision eternal damnation as his future, Michael pledges and breaks troth with Mary:

> But still the two affixed their hands and seals
> To a life compact witnessed by the sky,
> Where the great planets drove their glittering wheels,
> Bringing conflicting fate, making men die.

Neither is he remorseful in his indulgence: Fate rules the world. Man is not responsible for being, he argues: "I did not make myself; this life is often hell"; Furthermore,

> Hell is my future; I shall soon have died,
> But I will take to hell one memory more.

Notwithstanding Mary's legitimate union with another, the law of necessity that drove him to infidelity before, now leads him to offer her a violated honor; one of the bloody doorways they have made from their hell, the poet says, to cut their tangle. And when Fate had finished the tragic pattern, there lay

> Three blind ones, dear, . . . in the slough,
> Caught fast for death; but never mind that now.

"The Widow in the Bye Street" strongly stresses Fate as debtor of all on earth. When the element of chance might be read into the action of the story, the poet quickly interposes the belief that Fate determines the decision:

> Ev'n so stood life and death, and could not tell
> Whether she'd go to the inn and find her son,
> Or take the field and let the doom be done.

> She turned, and left the inn and took the path
> And "Brother Life, you lost," said Brother Death,

> "Even as the Lord of all appointed hath
> In this great miracle of blood and breath."

> He doeth all things well, as the book saith,
> He bids the changing stars fulfill their turn,
> His hand is on us when we least discern.

Whereas Masefield uses the term "Lord," nevertheless, he seems bewildered by the different terms, Providence and Fate. Presently, we shall find comment to support this theme.

"The Widow in the Bye Street" also develops the theory with the idea of the unexpected. Behold four souls and

> The dark, invisible hand of secret Fate
> Brought it to come to being that they met
> After so many years of lying in wait
> While we least think it he prepares his Mate.

Unhallowed love of three contests the devotion of a mother, surrenders fully to the moment lest the morrow should not come, and tastes the bitter poison Love puts "on Fate's arrow." When the arrow pierces, it is shot by the invisible hand that has prepared the bow for the widow's son back in the days, when as a little child, he shared her room. Fearing life, they fear death, yet, as the widow says,

> . . . it's the end of curses,
> A rest for broken things too broke to mend.

Again, the force of Fate rules in "The Everlasting Mercy." Saul Kane is a reformed drunkard. Early in life, he "was tokened to the devil." Wherefore, a life more or less of sin was his fate. Tempted to the extreme of suicide, as an escape from the inevitable in devilish promptings like:

> Why fret and swear and try to mend?
> It's all the same thing in the end.

> But when it's done, he said, it's ended.
> Why stand it since it can't be mended?

Nevertheless, he craved living to the full and resolved:

> I won't. I've never had my go.
> I've not had all the world can give.
> Death by and by, but first I'll live.
> The world owes me my time for times,
> And that time's coming now, by crimes.

Hence, he sinned gladly and irresponsibly, certain of mercy at the end: the more grievous the sin, the more beneficent would be Christ's mercy. Fate decrees the opportunity for the extension of forgiveness by a power which Masefield described above as

> . . . a great and lovely figure, beyond all sex, throned somewhere and crowned, to whom the sharp prayer might pierce.[5]

"Dauber" also reveals Masefield's fascination for fatalism. A young "dauber" sails the sea to learn to paint it as a sailor knows it. His talent is inherited from his mother on whose sketchings her husband poured the same discouragement which he showered on the boy's art. He allowed neither mother nor son a life of their own. They should have been farm lovers; instead they were failures. Repeated attempts at self-conquest followed only to realize that the farm was prison, "and, then I'd try awhile; but it was Fate." On shipboard his life approximated to failure: he was thought no man and no sailor. But one day inspiration came; he would be the world's interpreter of the men who fight the sea; he would do it through personal experience, for

> It was most proud, however self might doubt,
> To share man's tragic toil and paint it true.
> He took the offered Fate: this he would do.

Thereafter his soul, the poet says, was on probation. The Fate that made his former trials futile still prompts him to the thought:

> I'm a failure. All
> My life has been a failure. They were right.
> I'll never paint. Best let it end tonight.

Yet Fate is not to be unkind. He had prayed for release, but not before

> He had emerged out of the iron time,
> And knew that he could compass his life's scheme;
> He had the power sufficient to his dream.

That evil forces impel disaster by sea is Masefield's belief in "The Wanderer." Weathering storms, yet paying the toll of life or damage, the ship returned to dock always in tattered glory. Each new departure raised the query: what unseen power had prepared her harm? Ill-fated and cursed, it seems, she was deserted yet only for awhile. The "Wanderer" breasted the waves again while her crew sing life as a game in which the weak lose, a battle in which the strong win. "The River," too, presents occasion for the workings of Fate. Blows from Nature would suggest to the poet who had felt its every whim the inexorableness of Fate. Here are some fragments from the poem:

> They found that Fate had caught them in a pen,
> The door that opened out was jammed with wreck.
> And still the ship stood steady in the slime,
> While Fate above her fingered with her urn.
> Time's minute-hand had been the hand of Fate.

Even a horse-race can voice the doctrine of the poet. "Man who lives under sentence sealed," attended the fate of Right Royal and his rivals. And when

All the noise died behind, Fate was waiting in front,
Now the racing began, they had done with the hunt.[6]

In the midst of seemingly approaching defeat, the rider
makes a declaration worthy of fatalism:

My vision was wisdom, or the World as it is.
Fate rules us, not Wisdom, whose ways are not his,
Fate, weaponed with all things, has willed that I fall;
So be it, Fate orders, and we go to the wall.[7]

And in succeeding lines Masefield departs, as he seldom
does, from the absolute rule of Fate to say:

Yet, Royal, my comrade, before Fate decides,
His hand stays, uncertain, like the sea between tides,
Then a man has a moment, if he strike not too late,
When his soul shakes the world soul, and can even change
    Fate.

Obviously, this is opposed to the attitude generally maintained by Masefield. It rather echoes what the poet intimates when he wrote "Fate has his way with those who mar
what is decreed." He makes similar profession in the event
of rescuing a lady from the Caliph's power:

"If we fail,"
He said, It will be Fate, who flings the die
Against which nothing mortal can avail.
But we are desperate men whose throws succeed,
Being one with Fate, or Change from Passionate Need.[8]

None of the narratives of Masefield escapes from the
influence of predestination or Fate. Evil is always seen in
the perspective:

But this bright child is fated to such crime
As will make mark a bloody smear on Time.[9]

Life is an enigma. Whatever it may be,

> It is most great,
> Through blood and brain alone it wrestles Fate.[10]

"Badon Hill" consistently, in respect to the time of pagan England, holds the idea of Fatalism:

> He swore to raid there with a gang, but Fate
> That loves but ruins boldness, shut the gate.

In the lyric, "The Seekers," fatalism is still the dominant mood and tone. Masefield seems to be searching for the City of God, yet he does it as a fatalist: he is seeking what he says he will never find. Life offers but the hope to "search for a hidden city that we shall never see." More vital to this study is the lyric, "A Creed." Personally emotional, subjective, it is the man telling us of his faith in the theory, un-Catholic and un-Christian, of metempsychosis: reincarnation, a double fatalism, and, therefore, fatalism at its worst. He says:

> I hold that when a person dies
> His soul returns to earth;
> Arrayed in some new flesh-disguise
> Another mother gives him birth.
> With sturdier limbs and brighter brain
> The old soul takes the roads again.

The persistence of his soul in the new embodiment will effect a continued purgation

> Until this case, this clogging mould,
> Be smithied all to kingly gold.

Reference has been made to the poet's confused sense of Providence and Fate. Here and there he mistakes one for the other:

> Our Fates are strange, and no one knows his;
> Our lovely Saviour Christ disposes.[11]

> A quiet house, like all that God controls,
> It is Fate's instrument on human souls.[12]

> They had a death look, wild and odd,
> Of something dark foretold by God.[13]

Yet the disorder is an easy consequence of the bewilderment of his conception concerning God's identity:

> Is the Good God to Whom none calls in vain,
> Man's Achieved Good, which being Life, abides,
> The man-made God, that man in happy breath
> Makes in despite of Time and dusty death.[14]

To him nature is God, Christ is the plough of men's souls, and

> . . . the laughter
> Of holy white birds flying after.[15]

And then while he would seem to profess God as the Creator, he deviates to question what is the source of the nothingness, what its primal functionings, and what did it have of intelligence. Was it perhaps a Mind that fashioned mystery? Or was it merely chance accumulating and directing atoms? Was there a power, a blind law, or "conscious law"?

> Or a vast balance by vast clashes wrought
> Or Time at trial with Matter for an hour?[16]

From doubt he passes on to absolute denial and insists that Man's inherent bent to revere and adore is for "what he thinks the truth." Within the space of a sonnet he declares three times: "There is no God," and adds

> . . . but we, who breathe the air,
> Are God ourselves and touch God everywhere.[17]

This clearly is Pantheism: the creed of the individuals who believe that matter and its energies are God.

"The Everlasting Mercy," generally fatalistic, is essentially pantheistic as well. After his conversion, Saul Kane saw everything in nature as an emanation from God; even a brick ledge or a wild herb was a part of the essence of God. Both "were parts of an eternal glory." As a fugitive example we offer from one of his sonnets on life these lines:

> Thy god, the holy ghost, the atoning Lord,
> Here in the flesh, the never yet explored.[18]

Pantheism leads naturally to Immanentism, for if we are part of God, the powers of soul, thoughts, ideas come from the natural processes of the soul. Man is self-sufficient. Indisputably Masefield says this again here:

> Here in the self is all that man can know
> Of Beauty, all the wonder, all the power,
> All the unearthly color, all the glow,
> Here in the self which withers like a flower;
> Here in the self which fades as hours pass,
> And droops and dies and rots and is forgotten,
> Sooner, by ages, than the mirroring glass
> In which it sees its glory still unrotten.[19]

In another sonnet, in the sequence wherein he tries also to analyze existence, he arrives at the same conclusion of Immanentism that man, "a thing of watery salt, Held in cohesion by unresting cells," continues in being through his own parts working intrinsically. Other sonnets in the series reflect the theory crediting nature and creatures with powers not their own. In one he issues this challenge:

Is there a great green commonwealth of Thought
Which ranks the yearly pageant, and decided
How Summer's royal progress shall be wrought,
By secret stir which in each plant abides?

· · · ·

Does spotted cowslip with the grass agree
To hold her pride before the rattle burst?

· · · ·

Or is it, as with us, unresting strife,
And each consent a lucky gasp for life?[20]

The most recent poetry of Mr. Masefield is Christian in essence. "End and Beginning" is thoroughly Catholic: Mary of Scotland dies a martyr for her faith. *The Coming of Christ* is in the same orthodox tone, maintaining the Gospel story and acknowledging the Divinity of the Child. There is only one reference to Fate. That is voiced by the spirit of Christ in the line, "Earth with its death and Fate." Thus the poet clings to Fate, but it is a Fate bounded by earth. In his lyric, "A Creed," he professes it. Yet he holds to Pantheism also and to Immanentism, both as inner forces antithetic to Fate. And these forces proceed from God. Clearly the poet confuses Fate with God. The personality of God to him is simply the Unknown. Wherefore, he is the fatalist, because the creed of the fatalist is this, that an unknown force inexorably predetermines the actions of the individual. Through all Masefield's fatalism there runs the beautiful haunting hope that, as there is pity in Man's heart, there may somewhere beyond also be an everlasting mercy.

ROBINSON JEFFERS

Takes God to task

Extracts from
LETTER FROM ROBINSON JEFFERS

As to my "religious attitudes"—you know it is a sort of tradition in this country not to talk about religion for fear of offending—I am still a little subject to the tradition, and rather dislike stating my "attitudes" except in the course of a poem. However, they are simple. I believe that the universe is one being, all its parts are different expressions of the same energy, and they are all in communication with each other, influencing each other, therefore parts of one organic whole. (This is physics, I believe, as well as religion.) The parts change and pass, or die, people and races and rocks and stars; none of them seems to me important in itself, but only the whole. This whole is in all its parts so beautiful, and is felt by me to be so intensely in earnest, that I am compelled to love it, and to think of it as divine. It seems to me that this whole alone is worthy of the deeper sort of love; and that there is peace, freedom, I might say a kind of salvation, in turning one's affections outward toward this one God, rather than inward on one's self, or on humanity, or on human imaginations and abstractions—the world of spirits.

I think that it is our privilege and felicity to love God for his beauty, without claiming or expecting love from him. We are not important to him, but he to us.

I think that one may contribute (ever so slightly) to the beauty of things by making one's own life and environment beautiful, so far as one's power reaches. This includes moral beauty, one of the qualities of humanity, though

Tor House, Carmel, California.
October 1, 1934.

Dear Sister Mary James:

Your letter clauses have been answered honestly, but these have been too many vicissitudes and often comes the first foolishness.

As to my "religious attitude"—you know it—we talk about a sort of fatalism in this country not to make a little subject religion for fear of offending—you still a little subject to the vicissitudes, and matter, so like stating my attitude about ...

[remainder of letter in difficult handwriting]

Sincerely yours,
Robinson Jeffers.

it seems not to appear elsewhere in the universe. But I would have each person realize that his contribution is not important, its success not really a matter for exultation nor its failure for mourning; the beauty of things is sufficient without him.

(An office of tragic poetry is to show that there is beauty in pain and failure as much as in success and happiness.)

Oct. 1, 1934

FIVE

> I believe that the universe is one being, all its parts are different expressions of the same energy, and they are all in communication with each other, influencing each other, therefore parts of one organic whole . . . This whole is in all its parts so beautiful, and is felt by me to be so intensely in earnest, that I am compelled to love it, and to think of it as divine,

IN THESE words, Robinson Jeffers avows pantheism. To love God for His beauty, without hope of requital, is, he maintains, man's prerogative. Nevertheless, Jeffers takes God to task for not bettering the affairs of mankind. Science, new Russia, and poets are all builders: "they serve God, Who is very beautiful, but hardly a friend of humanity." This is the attitude of a Deist: belief in a God as apart from His creations (a belief opposed to pantheism) and as a Deity Who manifests no concern in the functions of his creatures. That Deity he finds not only "unkindly all but inhuman," indifferent to creatures, but "not moderate enough to trust, and when he turns bad, no one can bear him to the end."[1] Moreover, God is,

> . . . the sonorous
> Antistrophe of desolation to the strophe multitude.[2]

He "closes his hand over this house" and even avenges. Hence this censure from Jeffers:

> Is God's hand lamed?
>
> . . . . .
>
> What has God done? I had sons and loved them too much,
> And he is jealous.[3]

With the felicity man enjoys in loving God for His Beauty, there is also the privilege of sharing it to the fullest

extent of one's power. For those less gifted to rise to that
level the poet emphasizes that each person

> realize that his contribution is not important, its success
> not really a matter for exultation nor its failure for mourn-
> ing; the beauty of things is sufficient without him.

A deflection of the sentiments from the ego, an attitude of
an extrovert rather than that of an introvert, warrants not
only peace and freedom, but salvation. Jeffers would,
therefore, concentrate man's heart and mind on the world
of externals instead of on the world of spirit. He would go
farther: he would have man found a new religion. "All
religions are dead," he writes, "You are chosen to found
a new one, To draw from your own fountain the soul of
the world."[4]

"The Women at Point Sur" is symbolic of Robinson
Jeffers and his religious faith. Dr. Barclay, a minister, has
lost his trust in Protestantism: Christianity is false. That
Christ was God, that He died to redeem man, that He
rose from the dead is a fable. Barclay preaches that God
reveals Himself through action on the part of the individual, and that man does so similarly. Breaking faith with
revealed truth or tradition is "action." Murder is action
"not an inch more monstrous than any other." Man needs
only to give evidence of the ability to start in another
direction. Then one can justify the consequences with his
own reasons. In good or evil, God will reveal Himself.
Man will find Him in either of two ways:

> . . . gather disciples
> To fling like bullets against God and discover him
> Or else commit an act so monstrous, so irreparable
> It will stand like a mountain of rock, serve you for a
>   fulcrum
> To rest the lever. In vacancy: nothing.[5]

Barclay begins action with three questions: Is there a God? (If so, is He one?) Is there a hereafter? How should men live? His own mind directs him to confess

> . . . There is one Power,
> You may call it God to the vulgar.[6]

It is the god of Pantheism, as Jeffers states in his own letter, the

> God that grows up in trees and mountains, the same
>   power
> In the wrinkled limbs formed them and smoothed them,
>   drew them long, . . .
> Made beautiful the throat.[7]

All this, he declares,

> . . . is God's brain, the water, the cloud yonder,
> The coast hills, thinking the thing out to conclusion.[8]

He sees God in the dead grass of the hill, the crystal blue of the sea, the blood of man, the whiteness of stone, the blackness of water,—even in the toad. This one power that possesses all equally, he calls "God" to the people. Yet there are occasions when he blasphemes it: the "Enduring anima," he writes:

> You have no conception . . . of the treachery of what's
>   his name?—God, God.[9]

Allusions to the Sacrifice of the Mass are scurrilous in this poem as well as in others. He imagines

> A priest by the yet-twitching carcass of sacrifice
> Plunging his hands into the hot red cavern . . .[10]

Father O'Donnel, an old priest,

> Gabbles the Latin faster to an end and turns himself once
> more and says to the people, "Go home now. Missa est."[11]

Man, also, Jeffers takes to task. In "Intellectuals," he reproaches the masses for blindly following Marx, Christ, or mere Progress. Action he recommends from the individual. God, he charged, is too secure to want worshipers. He includes the sheep with the wolves,

> . . . the flaming stars and pitiable flesh,
> And what we call things and what we call nothing.[12]

Then, too, God gives no solace to men as they trudge their way to the goal of despair, tire of the struggle, blind themselves to the light, and flock into the fold.

In the progress of "The Women at Point Sur," Jeffers solves his second query: Is there a hereafter? At first, assured that death ends all, that "the after is trash,"

> Annihilation, the beautiful crystal contrivance
> To catch rays from outside the stars in,[13]

he enjoys a change of heart and seems to hear the white fibers of the hill whispering that they are one with God. Wherefore, he arrives at the belief that "annihilation's impossible, the dead have none." Man will go on, he will be God, "he is inexhaustible." The pantheistic notion resides in his "Inscription for a Gravestone": man will assume the essence of Beauty as an ethereal element for he will

> Touch you and Asia
> At the same moment; have a hand in the sunrises
> And the glow of this grass.

With respect to the third inquiry: "How shall man live?" Jeffers makes adequate answer: God thinks through action. Accordingly, all law is abolished; the sanction is, too. The action makes for deliverance; it discovers God. In the interval,

There is nothing wicked, nothing strange in the world.
What the heart desires, . . .
That is the law. The God of the stars has taken his hand
    out of the laws and has dropped them empty
As you draw your hand out of a glove.[14]

What one does is nothing. No act is a sin. God gives no commandment. Hence,

That you *be* your desires, break custom, flame, flame,
Enter freedom.[15]

Yet whatever man does, he does because he is fated. He is a mere pawn in the hands of God, fickle, frivolous, and merciless. Christ Himself, so Jeffers feels, scorns the circumstances of man's serving "the triumphant occasions of God." But when Judas attains to the calling of betrayal foreplanned him by the Master, and bitterly upbraids Him with

You teach mercy: be merciful. . . . To let the people alone is the mercy . . . I know by heart that agate inflexible look in his eyes. There is no hope in this merciless man.[16]

the Christ defends the seeming fate with

I tell you feelingly, it is the honor of all men living to be dupes of God.[17]

In the honor there is inevitable destiny. Jeffers makes Deity proclaim it:

Listen to me now, Judas, and remember.
Because I know your scrupulous heart, and I don't wish
    you to die despairing. There is not one creature,
Neither yourself nor anyone, nor a fly nor flung stone,
    but does exactly and fatally the thing
That it needs must; neither less nor more.[18]

Wherefore, all mankind falls into a net. And the mind of

Jeffers allows even Christ Himself to be so ensnared: He chooses His own fate and in so doing, destines the treason of the apostle. "Dear Judas," then, is one of Jeffers' major rebukes to Omnipotence. Nor does he let it rest at that. While he praises, he dispraises:

> The world's God is treacherous and full of unreason;
> a torturer, but also
> The only foundation and the only fountain.[19]

Creation is victimized always. The ether, the hills, and man in particular are the sport of a pitiless God Whom Jeffers will often take to task.

BOOK TWO: SEEKERS AFTER GOD

Edwin Arlington Robinson:

The first of the seekers

Dear Madam:

While the matter is certainly settled for you, as a good Catholic, there is room for an infinite amount of groping and searching for many who cannot accept the tenets of your Church, or of any other. It is evident that science is not giving, for a good many, at any rate, any satisfactory substitute for religion, which is perhaps becoming more and more a thing for each one to feel for himself. I should say too you might find many evidences of this in recent verse.

Yours sincerely,

(Signed) E. A. Robinson

January 21, 1930

328 East 42 Street
New York, January 21, 1930

Dear Madam,

While the matter is certainly
settled for you, as a good Catholic,
there is room for an infinite amount
of groping and searching for many
who cannot quite accept the whole
of your Church, or of any other.
It is evident that science is not
giving, for a great many, at any
rate, any satisfactory substitute
for religion, which is perhaps
becoming more and more a thing
for each one to find and feel
for himself. I should say that
you might find many evidences
of this in recent works.

Yours sincerely

E. A. Robinson

To Sister Mary James
Waltham, Mass

SIX

A MEMBER of no church, an observer of no ritual, a believer in no creed, Edwin Arlington Robinson did not completely ignore religion. He formulated his own. Rejecting revealed religion and the teaching of a visible church, alone he sought Truth. His quest refuted any tendency to agnosticism, for he thereby denied his inability to know with certainty. It refuted, as well, any charge of fatalism, for he seems to have acknowledged a higher divinity. That divinity he usually called "God." Into the mouth of some of his characters, he put the name "fate," but he seldom capitalized it.

His search, therefore, places him definitely among those for whom religion means "an infinite amount of groping and searching." They are, he tells the writer, the "many who cannot quite accept the tenets of your Church or of any other." Yet, feeling that some formula of faith is of vital necessity in this changing age, he makes this comment:

> Outside the Catholic Church, religion is having a pretty hard time nowadays.
> It is evident that science is not giving, for a good many, at any rate, any satisfactory substitute for religion, which is becoming more and more a thing for each to find or feel for himself.

He implies this similar inadequacy of science to minister unto the eternal in man when he upbraids Matthias for his lack of penetration.

> There's more of you for you to find, Matthias,
> Than science has found yet, or may find soon.
> Science that blinds its eyes incessantly,

73

With a new light that fades and leaves them aching,
Whatever it sees, will be a long time showing
To you, Matthias, what you have striven so hard
To see in the dark.[1]

Morally consoling science may be to those who would deify the cell, yet through more inspiring founts than chemistry does the water of Truth flow upon the human soul in spiritual crises. Is the good atheist always unbelieving? Does not a manifest fear make plain a doubt repudiating nothing as the beginning and the end of our existence? May not the reputed man of science in an unguarded moment, weary of negation and haphazard chance, confronted with the real, see Truth and see it almost whole? Speaking of Nightingale possessing everything and yet fearing everything, Robinson says,

A tired bacteriologist, seeing him there,
Might say there was a God, Nature, at least,
Had never done her work so well before,
Or saved a man of science so much trouble.[2]

Further reflection the poet makes through "The Man Against the Sky," a Dantesque study on man facing eternity. There, as the universal man stands on the outermost rim of earth, the questionings are many. Courage struggles with cowardice. Vision contends with despair. Reason fights with faith. But hope rises to triumph. Are we never to hear the one Living Word because, earthbound and fettered, "Eternity records Too vast an answer for the time-born words We spell . . ." Will the race of man be the plaything for the hand of Science? Contrariwise, reason will not long so control the mind to the belief that man has been made merely to fill a trap and thus pass on to nothingness. Will we not survive the echo or

> . . . the noise we make
> Along one blind atomic pilgrimage
> Whereon by crass chance billeted we go
> Because our brains and bones and cartilage
> Will have it so?

Faith, then, lights the poet's path more clearly than science directs his reason. Without its glimmer, at least, there would be endless night; there would be night of constant gloom. Without some sensation of God, joy is the light hid under a bushel. But the consciousness of Divinity makes the tiresome untiring. Otherwise there is

> . . . nothing to do them for. You have your God—
> If you have not forgotten him and lost him—
> But I have nothing. Do you hear me? Nothing.[3]

Thus Nathalie complains to Matthias who, in later questioning after her death, is to deny belief in all beyond the sense of nature. Reason alone can tear away the veil that keeps man in the dark. So protests Matthias, who, as Nathalie said once "had God," only to hear this as a deciding counter-force from the man Robinson:

> Hold fast, Matthias.
> There's not a man who breathes and believes nothing.
> So you are done with mysteries. If you are,
> You are the one elected and fulfilled
> Initiate and emeritus of us all.[4]

Providence and Its Infinite Ways are not always in heavy relief to man's understanding. Yet there is some impression, for the least faith embosses it. Dr. Quick thinks so, as he envies the good he might have done in the ministry where he might have reclaimed from the way of evil men who had digressed from the dispensations of God, unfelt and unseen by the many without the supersense of faith. To them,

> . . . His laws are said
> To be obscure; yet my belief in them
> Uncovers them, and sees them occupied
> Not far from where we live. They are outside
> The kingdom of our wits . . .[5]

To those laws Robinson pays his tribute by submission. Being human, doubts and fears must sometimes harass him but never will they wholly swerve him. He will not interfere with God's appointed ways with him. He will give as much as God would ask of him. His desire will be in the proportion of God's gift. What God does he will conform to happily. Speaking in Timberlake, he says: "For me, I'll trust the chances. I shall not go until my name is called." And in old Isaac when he said: "When we are done with all but the Divine, We die." Death is the beginning, he intimates, of what will merit more the "Jubilate" than the dirge.

And before all that which means liberation from the unhappy here, a lasting home, will come a judgment day presided over by a God as scrutinizing as He is merciful now in withholding from the mortal mind the day and the hour when man will cease to live.

> Is it not God's first mercy
> To suffering man that he shall not know when?
> Why do you ask for more than you would know?[6]

God's Wisdom is in the order of His mercy. It is infinite. Robinson would have Ponce de Leon realize the Omniscience of God in defeating his plans to discover the fountain that would bring not only perpetual youth, but the fulfilment of evil propensities long a part of him. Through Nightingale, too, the poet says:

> God in His Wisdom, which is infinite,
>   And is not ours, has always made such things
> To be consumed . . .[7]

Laramie reminds Cavender, when his frenzied mind conjures her spiritual presence before him, that death may be near upon him, Tonight, perhaps, she warns. He has lived long enough, she thinks. And a meaningless ejaculation, "God knows it's time," brings out a salient truth not meant to be colloquial: "Unless he knows that you must go on living." Fargo twice admits God as the Source of all Knowledge. Why he is here, he does not know, but God knows. Reasoning with himself can add nothing else than

> '. . . I have not done
> Large evil in the world where I belong;
> I am not here for that; I am not here
> By wilful choice, by call, or by command
> That I remember.'[8]

The Divinity that shapes our ends is omnipotent. Malory was like God, so Nightingale thought, for "He was omnipotent." The whole world is His, because He made it. God made Evensong generous, he thinks. Atlas knows God gave him vision. Another seems to think God fears the monsters of his own creation. If not, why should He conceal them in the depths of ocean beds? Was it His Foresight or His Love that submerged the hideous from man? They do neither harm nor good. God and His Ways are inscrutable. Although we are "incarnate . . . in God's image," does any of God's creation know less of what we are than we? However, this with certainty, in the midst of the search for truth,

> . . . why do we shun to know
> That in Love's elemental over-glow
> God's wholeness gleams with light superlative?
> .   .   .   .   .
> Look at a branch, a bird, a child, a rose,
> Or anything God ever made that grows,—

> Nor let the smallest vision of it slip,
> Till you may read, as on Belshazzar's wall,
> The glory of eternal partnership.[9]

All is in God: our birth, our succeeding years, and our death. Hence, our dependence wholly upon Him, Robinson tells us in "The Garden." Life, he knows, is a garden. And in his introspection, in company with the Gardener, he has gone through it, seeing all the many flowers and the weeds. Among the flora he saw his own deeds: "sad weeds," they were his life. He saw the lives of everybody there. Propagated they had been from the seeds of eternity; rooted they were in God's Love and tended by His guidance. All through the garden was a sense of otherworldliness, essential principles, those things of the spirit touching the chords in man's heart naturally vibrant to the eternal verities:

> That Love's complete communion is the end
> Of anguish to the liberated man.[10]
>
> .   .   .   .   .
>
> We shriek to live, but no man ever lives
> Till he has rid the ghost of human breath.[11]

The mysterious presence of the everlasting Robinson seemed to feel as a child. A house with beauty hovering round in fragrance and in the cool of dew suggested to him in those early years the splendor of the supernatural. It seemed to echo with the voices of those whispering now in eternity. The same intuition lets him hear now as then such preludes. They sound as music not of earth. Will their transcendent notes roll on to spheres of rarer aura? The poet says it is music attuned to "some vast harmony that no brief mortal touch has ever stirred." This melody entirely alien to any string played on by man, this ecstasy of heavenly vibrations will go on for

> . . . after time and place are overthrown,
> God's touch will keep its one chord quivering.[12]

That music one enjoys through the faithful observance
of God's Laws. Little children bless the world with music
that will always keep a city within the sight of God. A man
to win eternal favor must be a child again, in spirit not in
deed, he says, to sanctify if not to save one's soul. Again,
to keep the music sounding, the gold of charity must
redeem another's faults and failings. To do otherwise is to
love the darkness more than the light, to listen to Caiphas
rather than to Nicodemus, to gibe the Master as we did
nineteen hundred years ago. And here in this allusion, the
poet recalling Calvary cries out:

> Tell me, O Lord,—tell me, O Lord, how long
> Are we to keep Christ writhing on the cross![13]

How long? He intimates the time: Christ will not be
vindicated for His sufferings on the Cross until the last
day when His enemies shall be made His footstool. This is
belief, orthodox, Christian, as when Robinson says, speaking as Paul and not Saul of Tarsus, that faith without love
is vain, that the living man is the man within himself, the
soul, and that the best in life is that which we can never
know. God speaks, so John Brown says, sometimes to a
soul in time of need, but

> . . . Most of us never know—
> And there you have a reason to believe
> In God, if you may have no other.[14]

Loving the spiritual, believing in the Providence of
God, hampered, as he must have thought, by no dogma,
Robinson lived by the promptings of a heart that was
purely Christian. Captain Craig's philosophy is Robin-
sonian. Far removed it is from the Pilgrim Mothers' ances-

tors of Althea, who tells that they measured God's Love by
their toil, their sober and sequestered lives. Captain Craig
has the humaneness of Christ, not the austerity of the
Puritans. He estimated as value not anything material but
the "inward eye for the dim face Of what this dark world
is." He counted not the gift but the heart of the giver.
He impressed that a triumph is never reached alone, nor
did he ever fall alone, neither did he reach real joy until
he learned "to laugh with God."

Singing the Christlike in spirit and in deed, Edwin
Arlington Robinson was an idealist, believing in his fellowmen and reconciling their apparent failures with success.
Loss of faith in man or in oneself is less endurable, he says,
than loss of faith in God.

> . . . For one who has once had it,
> . . . Losing his faith in God is a disaster
> By doubt still clouded and by nature made
> Supportable.[15]

Here Robinson's faith flickers rather than flames. Nor is
the circumstance an occasional one. While he believes in
God, attributes to Him powers of the Deity, still all his
years were searching ones. But they were hopeful ones.
When Cavender retired into a scene charged with memories
of the past, charged so, that he could speak with the presence of his departed Laramie, she answers reassuringly his
questions that may have been the poet's:

> 'Is there a God?'
> . . . 'Is there a Purpose, or a Law?'
>
> .   .   .   .   .
>
> 'Yes there is hope,'
> She said, as if with a prepared reluctance,
> 'Always except in those infernal words
> Over the gates of hell—which, after all,
> Are only man's invention. . . .[16]'

And when Robinson chants his credo: that all is maze for him, that light does not even flicker, and that no voice calls, hope rises and he feels the coming glory of the Light. In "The Pilot," too, one hears the search being made always alone. One hears, as well, the note of complementing hope for, in the absence of his inspiration, the poet still sails on.

Significant of the poet's search for Truth is his repeated use of the word "grope." Furthermore, he has used it in a letter to the writer. Note these at hand:

> Between your groping and the towers of God[17]
>
> .   .   .   .   .
>
> . . . You have
> A right to blind me with your mysteries,
> And one to see me groping, as I am now . . .[18]
>   . . . He was tired
> Of deserts, and found at last that his,
> Where he had groped and stumbled for so long[19]
> . . . and now pride was tired
> Of groping with Matthias among shadows.[20]

This groping for Truth, as has been said before, vindicates Robinson from the position of a fatalist. He does make fugitive remarks as when he says:

> . . . So Malory must be fate,
> Or more than fate, doing God's work, or fate's
> Or whatsoever the best name of it
> Might be;[21]

"Fate," here, is no First Cause revered by Robinson. Nor when he says, "Some chemistry of fate, forestalling him," although he may misuse even "destiny" so far to tell Samuel Talifer that his mother "was prepared by destiny . . . to fulfil" his father's life, for, in a similar instance, Robinson "assumes it was God's way." Far removed from pagan fatalism is his harmonizing of Divine prescience with human liberty. Besides, the poet would have good come from the hand of God in merit for man's observance of the moral law. And there, as hereinbefore, he would exonerate himself of fatalism which denies free will. And here he makes it clearer; in a cat personified as Ampersand, he makes this statement:

> . . . He was flying to his fate,
> And here was I, ordained to swallow him.
>
>   .   .   .   .   .
>
> Nature in us
> Is more intractable and peremptory;
> Wherefore you call us feral and ferocious,
> Which is unfair to us; for the same God
> Who sees a sparrow on the ground shows us
> The way to catch him, and we cannot choose.
> You can, you say . . .[22]

Robinson we place among the seekers after God through a knowledge attained only by conviction. Like himself, the characters of his poems, purely dramatic studies, are searching, too. Their quest seems never ended. Why? Because of each, as of himself, Robinson might say what he has said of "Cavender's House": "As in the Lord's house, there are many mansions, And some that he has not so much as opened, Having so much to learn."[23]

EDWIN MARKHAM:

The prophet of a kingdom coming

EDWIN MARKHAM

My religion is based on my profound faith in Jesus—in the reality of his life and in the lofty idealism of his teaching. He stirred all of Palestine into a ferment of hope, into a fire of devotion—into a fire of devotion to Him and into a hope for the new industrial order he called The Kingdom.

This was the first time in human history that this enthusiasm, this hunger for Brotherhood, took fire among the people. Jesus had this deep divine brotherhood in mind when he came preaching: "The Kingdom of Heaven is at hand—repent and accept the Kingdom."

To establish this Kingdom of Brothers, with a material and economic basis, this was the supreme purpose in the life and teaching of the holy master. This social purpose is the one music that sounds out of all his lofty idealism in The Sermon on the Mount.

Yes, there is one immense passion in Jesus of Nazareth. It is the passion of Fraternity, for in Fraternity is the essence of all gospels and the fulfilment of all revelations. In Fraternity men would find the key to unlock the problem of Labor and Capital, the problem of the world's poverty and sorrow. Men are now standing in selfish and therefore unhappy relations to one another. In Fraternity, men would be brought at last into brotherly relations with one another and therefore into divine revelations. Fraternity in Christ is the divine purpose. If we would have a Christian Civilization we must change the world: we must make Government the organ of Fraternity.

SEVEN

EDWIN MARKHAM is the Prophet of a Kingdom Coming. The kingdom that he foretells is to be established when all men will be "inbrothered." Then will they live for and not on one another; they will love one another not only as much as themselves, but more than themselves. The Kingdom of Christ will have come upon earth to make the world one vast Brotherhood of Man, a Fraternal State, governed by Love radiating from the Divine Christ Who is its centre.

Markham's attitude toward religion is, therefore, one of belief in an industrial and social federation that man should organize here upon earth, a confraternity that enjoins no faith in rigid dogma, but, on the contrary, functions through the spirit of Christianity only. In a quatrain, the poet sings his credo:

> Here is the Truth in a little creed,
> Enough for all the roads we go:
> In Love, is all the law we need,
> In Christ, is all the God we know.[1]

That is the essence of Swedenborgianism. To the followers of Swedenborg, the seer of the eighteenth century, there is one God, in whom there is a Divine Trinity: He is the Lord Jesus Christ. They are saved by believing in Him, by avoiding evil because it is of and from the Devil, by doing good actions because they are of and from God, and by doing them as a man from himself, yet, believing at the same time, that they are done from the Lord with him and by him. These seminal principles one finds in the work of Edwin Markham. In verification, we quote his acknowledgment of Swedenborg's philosophy:

I wish to express my gratitude for the vast light that his teaching has shed upon my mind and upon all my volumes of verse.[2]

As an adherent of Swedenborg, Markham believes, also, that the highest expression of God is in man. That faith is the foundation of Markham's Utopia, his Brotherhood of Man. Early in life the vision of that Utopia came to him. Through the economic and social injustice that he saw befogging the world, it burned its image on his heart. Millet's painting of the toiler, misshapen by the greed of the few, awakened him to the outrage committed against the divine in man, and he responded with "The Man with the Hoe," a loud rebuke to overpowering Capitalism:

> O Masters, lords and rulers in all lands,
> Is this the handiwork you give to God,
> This monstrous thing distorted and soul-quenched?
> How will you ever straighten up this shape;
> Touch it again with immortality.

As Markham visions the Kingdom Coming, he sees always in proximity and in outstanding contrast the conditions of labor working toward a Nemesis. So far removed from the spirit of the Gospel of the Labor Christ, in Whom he sees the Ideal of Fraternity, are men who discover work not a blessing but a curse,

> For the toilers have the least,
> While the idlers lord the feast.
> Yes, our workers they are bound,
> Pallid captives to the ground;
> Jeered by traitors, fooled by knaves,
> Till they stumble into graves.[3]

Everywhere in society is there the plunder of the many by the few. The haggard faces of the poor look out upon the world of plenty. The toiler hangs upon the "Cross of Labor." Humiliated men receive no merited rest, and traitors misspend His Bread. Yet in the prospect of the Fraternal State, Markham sees a New Heaven and a New Earth, when the Brotherhood of Man, the working form for Christ on earth, will right all wrongs. Service to others, Love in Action, will be its act of homage to its White Comrade,

> Sweeter are comrade kindnesses to Him
> Than the high harpings of the Seraphim.[4]

But now, in time, even among the lower forms of life, he finds his ideal of Brotherhood. The ants, he observes, "bound by gentle Brotherhood," working with gay and busy toil, evenly distribute the yield; men, he observes, "shriveled up with hates," sharing unequal burdens, plunder the profits. Similarly, the birds prefigure the equality that will dominate the Kingdom. In contrast to the dispiritedness that he senses among builders who are constructing a spacious hall nearby, he hears the rapturous song of the throstles as they build their nests. Trees, furthermore, stand on an equal footing on the floor of God's kingdom, sharing their leafy comfort with all God's children, representing the plan of the Great Designer for democracy among men,

> . . . since the first star they have stood
> A testament of Brotherhood.[5]

Despite the apparent triumph of the Capitalist that Markham notes contrary to the principles of the Federation of Man, Labor has a dedicated patroness. Revering the Swedenborgian tenet of the Brotherhood, that "God is man absolute," she wears for her crown the passion-flower, and she stands beside the nail-torn God. Hearing the lamentations of nations oppressed, she breaks the infamous chain with which Greed has bound the earth. She is the Light in Darkness, the Muse of Labor. To dispel the evil of the centuries that men may dream of "The Kingdom of Fraternity foretold," is her sacred mission. And she performs it in the spirit of high joy, for she says that she is song. Wherefore, she warms the heart of man, when, in the midst of almost broken hopes, he hears her sing:

> I am Religion and the Church I build
>   Stands on the sacred flesh with passion packed;
> In me the ancient gospels are fulfilled—
> In me the symbol rises into Fact.[6]

Still he hopes for more tangible protection against the foe of his Ideal that will dominate the twentieth century. Along the road of the century there will watch a new Sphinx, Labor, that will ask the dreaded question and demand an answer or the destruction of the Brotherhood. Thus, he awaits a leader, one who will "Fill the labor throne and build the Comrade Kingdom, stone by stone."[7]

Early in life Markham declared faith in divine intervention to direct the ways of universal brotherhood. The Desired One, long since sung in prophecy by Isaiah, the One Who was to come to Israel, Whose name "shall be called Wonderful, Counsellor, The Mighty God, the everlasting Father, the Prince of Peace," is, he knows, the Desire of Nations. Prophet-like, he visions the Star of Hope that will reappear this time to shine upon a hero-world standing beneath the unfurled standard of Fraternity. But the promise in the sky will not herald the advent of the Glory of the Lord, veiled in a Child or in the pomp of a Hero-King preached by "tedious argument and milkless creed,"

> But in the passion of the heart-warm deed
>   Will come the Man Supreme.
> Yea, for He comes to lift the Public Care—

To build on Earth the Vision hung in air.
This is the one fulfillment of His Law—
The one Fact in the mockeries that seem
This is the Vision that the Prophets saw—
The Comrade Kingdom builded in their dream.[8]

That the coming of the Kingdom, despite the seeming fading of the Vision among men whose hearts are held by the meshes of gain, is inevitable, Markham impresses through its Divine origin. He says that "the vast in-brothering of man—the glory of the universe" began with time. Uninterruptedly the purpose has moved down through the centuries, unwavering in its determination to establish justice. The idea has been the music of the spheres; it was the song of the shepherds on that first Christmas night when reverberating the heavenly messengers they might have sung the Kingdom that had come in Mary's Child. For He came in the spirit of Brotherhood, an elder Brother, "a Common Man at home with cart and crooked yoke." And throughout His earthly mission, he preached the gospel of the New Republic. His Sermon on the Mount is the essence of the Kingdom.

That fundamental principle embodied in the Master's teaching: All things unto all men, Markham uses in specific examples for the progress of his State. Ivan, the watchman of Moscow, sharing his coat with the beggar, Elizabeth, who forgot herself in brother-love, and Hilary who "flung the psalter by and hurried to a brother's cry," are all the gospelers of the prophet who has formulated this, another creed for the members of his Utopia:

There is a destiny that makes us brothers:
   None goes his way alone:
All that we send into the lives of others
   Comes back into our own.[9]

And in the same key, the stories of Oswald's beneficence to the hungry of his realm, the gold that accused the king of wrong done to his people, the guest that came to Conrad, and the Juggler of Touraine who gave in worship to Mary his all, "fingers and body and feet," are parables sufficient to interpret the Kingdom that Markham prophesies. Functioning through men united in a Leader Whose "Esse" is infinite love, it is by virtue of this all-embracing charity that the Kingdom must be perpetual. Contrariwise, history records cities built and deeds done for a single glory merely. And where Tyre and Babylon, Greece and Rome, Thebes, Troy, and Carthage were, was felt once to be eternity, but time has taught the truth that

> No house can stand, no kingdom can endure
> Built on the crumbling rock of Self-Desire:
> Nothing is Living Stone, nothing is sure,
> That is not whitened in the social Fire.[10]

Fired with the hope of those heroes who have felt with the poet that the Vision cannot fail, Markham would conscribe all to the Dream. Like Lincoln, Mazzini, Lamennais, St. Francis, and even Cromwell, who have been of "The company of souls supreme," Americans have a special vocation in the Brotherhood. Other nations, he feels, are not privileged to have been held, as it were, in the hollow of God's Hand to carry out the Divine Will. From "The Errand Imperious" comes the voice to America:

> 'Tis yours to bear the World-State in your dream,
> To strike down Mammon and his brazen breed,
> To build the Brother-Future, beam on beam;
> Yours, mighty one, to shape the Mighty Deed.

As a tribute to her policy of arbitrating with rival states in South America and of commemorating the occasion

with an heroic statue of Christ surmounting the highest
peak of the Andes, Markham dedicates a prayer in verse
to the Divine Pacificator, imploring for the world on the
eve of the great war this protection:

> O Christ of Olivet, you hushed the wars
> Under the far Andean stars:
> Lift now your strong nail-wounded hands
> Over all peoples, over all lands:
> Stretch out those comrade hands to be
> A shelter over land and sea![11]

The war itself, entirely opposed to his Ideal of Brotherhood, the Federation of the Peoples, the Parliament of
Man, moved him to frequent utterance for peace through
the mediation of Love and Justice. These fragmentary
lines are significant:

> Peace, peace, O men, for you are brothers all—
>
> .   .   .   .   .
>
> Do you not know you came
> Out of one Love and wear one sacred name?[12]
> Comrades, read out His words again:
> They are the only hope for men!
> Love and not hate must come to birth;[13]
> Christ and not Cain must rule the earth.

And in the Red Cross League he saw the kindness and the
mercy that symbolize that league of infinite kindness
which will be "In ages when the agonies are done, When
all will love and all will lift as one."

Time has not weakened the prophet in Markham. To
him the Kingdom built on democracy and comrade-love
shines as the morning star of eternity. Quoting Laplace,
he holds that despite all the findings in science, one thing
alone remains: Love that constitutes the pillars of his State.
It is the self-subsisting force of the universe. Through it

Christ became divine, "having no self to serve, no will
That does not seek the welfare of All." This is truly
Swedenborgian philosophy. And the prophet would extend
it even to the realms of romance and call it the "Romance
of the Infinite"; He would take his "winged mate" beyond
the natural and cry out to his soul in the spirit of Gethsemane's great Love, "The Heart's Cry,"

> Can you be true to Love in spite of all,
>   Be true as granite in the mountain wall?

while the answer to the question self-imposed is the prayer
that he

> . . . shall stand full-armed in life's last hours—
> In the great night of death white and tall.[14]

This, too, is Swedenborgian in that all must be done for
the sake of Love alone. Nor does the thought of Heaven
as a reward influence the motive of the deed.

At eighty, the poet injected other specifically Swedenborgian philosophy. Adoring the Lord Christ not according to orthodox belief but as the embodiment of the
Trinity, he emphasized the "nail-torn Christus" as the
Omnipotent One, departing from the dogma of God as
the Provident Father. And the quatrain which is the
epitome of his gospel of the Parliament of Man plays likewise into the tenets of the philosophy by such a title as
"The New Trinity" by its suggestive refutation:

> Three things must a man possess if his soul would live,
>   And know life's perfect good—
> Three things would the all-supplying Father give—
>   Bread, Beauty and Brotherhood.

His interpretation of Heaven is from Swedenborg as
well: It is a real world reached only by those who have

passed through the preparatory schools of the angels. There also souls experience the long drama of Love, for heaven rests on the two great loves—the marriage love and the fraternal love. Fugitive lines like these carry the thought:

> A little while men eat this earthly bread,
> Then pass on to the nations of the dead.

> To the austere sifting of the vanisht crowds,
> Till on some souls the eternal sleep is shed.
> No, not immortal but immortable.[15]

> For she will be immortally my own—
> Mine in the marriage of eternity.[16]

At eighty, also, the prophet is inspired by another toiler. A reflection on Rodin's statue, "The Thinker," reimmortalizing labor, harks back to Markham's first thoughts in verse to celebrate the Brotherhood and elicits the daring line, "How patient he has been with God!" It leads on to a consideration of the same theme, reversing the subject to the oppressor when Markham as the prophet, scanning the streets and finding only consequences of self-love among all: the clergy and the laity, asks

> Who would welcome the Workman in,
> This Workman from Nazareth?[17]

Fittingly many poems of his last book, *Eighty Songs at Eighty*, are a prospect and a retrospect over all he has sung, for in essence he sings that the Kingdom is coming and that

> The crest and crowning of all good,
> Life's final star, is Brotherhood.[18]

Though the poet feels the glow of the Brotherhood of Man, unfortunately he does not enjoy the warmth of intimacy with a Personal God in Whom all things are one.

VACHEL LINDSAY

Chants a gospel of rapture for mankind

Extracts from

SECOND LETTER FROM ELIZABETH CONNOR LINDSAY

Your inquiry as to Mr. Lindsay's religious point of view is very easily answered. Mr. Lindsay violently repudiates the implication of Puritanism, though it is frequently hurled at him. I can understand why, for personally, and in his immediate background, the Puritanic and Victorian attitude toward life and its problems, is predominant. However, his ancestry does not include any of New England, which is what he means but is Virginian, Kentuckian, and homespun midwestern.

As a young man, he led the life of a Buddhist monk during his begging years; and as an art student in New York, before that time, he spent most of his devotional hours at the Church of the Paulist Fathers. These influences are apparent in many of his shorter poems. His family have belonged, however, ever since its foundation, to the church of the Disciples of Christ, otherwise known as the Christians, or the Campbellites, a Protestant denomination founded by Alexander Campbell, who was a Scotch Presbyterian before he caught a new vision.

Mr. Lindsay's maternal grandfather was a country squire who preached on Sundays; his mother was a devoted churchwoman: he went to Hiram College, a Campbellite school in Ohio; we have Alexander Campbell's portrait hanging in our parlor (one still has parlors in the Middle West!) where he is frequently taken for an ancestor, which he isn't, except in the spirit. You will find a group of

LINDSAY
603 SOUTH FIFTH STREET
SPRINGFIELD, ILLINOIS
U.S.A.

January 13, 1930

Dear Sister Mary James,

Mr. Lindsay asks me
to say to you that he voluntarily
in agreement with your evaluation.
Perhaps the best statement of
his position in that respect
is to be found in Theodore
Maynard's "Our Best Poets",
the chapter on Lindsay which
you doubtless know. Perhaps
the most helpful meaning
of Mr. Lindsay's religious
verse is "General Booth" —
where, in spite of the crude
external matter, one gets
a real spiritual feeling of

the meaning I indicate. The
poem gives one a triumph
over despair and always —
and was religious in its
origin. Then there is "I
Heard Immanuel Singing"
a material never really
a vision — and certainly
without loss of spiritual
feeling, now I those poems
I mention could have come to
us. Go on at student in New
York, Mr. Lindsay was not
a member of the church, spent
much time in the Protestant father
church — and once more is
"Lord yon Way I do" and
others speak loudly of that.
Can that help? I hope so!

With every good wish, I am
Yours most sincerely,
Elizabeth Lindsay
(Mrs. Vachel Lindsay)

poems on Alexander Campbell in the COLLECTED
POEMS; and you may be interested to know, too, that
Mr. Lindsay's sister, Olive, with her husband, Dr. Paul
Wakefield, spent twenty-five years on the foreign mission
field in China.

Mr. Lindsay still attends the church in which he was
baptized as a little boy, and which his mother and father
helped to build. He is liberal in his religious views, a stu-
dent of world religions, and perhaps more devoted to his
church because of associations than anything else; what-
ever the reason, the devotion is there. When he travels,
which is a great deal of the time, he finds himself invariably
seeking the open door and the altar light of your church,
as do many, I think, who have not yet found the way home.
But you asked for tangible facts, and such speculation
opens the way for the intangible.

October 3, 1931

EIGHT

WHETHER Lindsay sings to Gloriana or ushers Booth into heaven, the motive passion of his soul is one of rapture. In that spirit he chants the gospel that he felt himself missioned to preach. This gospel he chanted along the highways of the Middle West with all the rapture and enthusiasm of a circuit rider preaching religion:

> I come to you penniless and afoot to bring a message. I am starting a new religious idea. The idea does not say 'No' to any creed that you have heard . . . After this, let the denomination to which you now belong be called in your heart 'The Church of Beauty' or 'The Church of the Open Sky.'[1]

Wholly absorbed by the spirit of rapture, Lindsay preaches, as the vital principle of his new creed, the love of beauty. It is a vague creed, the love and worship of beauty. But in it the poet sees the love of God. There is the end of his search.

This shadowy doctrine, these almost meaningless words, so undefined that their meaning is limitless, Lindsay attained perhaps from his wanderings in the spiritual life in various sects. Selecting without any logical basis, accepting one thought through emotion and another through the beauty that he read into or from it, he had always been eclectic in his religious interest. Originally a member of the Church of the Disciples of Christ, "he was faithful more through associations than from conviction. On the road, exchanging his songs for bread and lodging, he lived the life of a Buddhist monk." He read deeply in Swedenborg whose principles he incorporated in his "Gospel of Beauty."

99

Lindsay's essential simplicity brought out high rapture. Thus his close friend, Paul Wakefield, said: "Lindsay never outgrew his lace-valentine days." They inspired him not only to the lyric, pleading sheltering and direction of young and innocent love:

> Were I a priest of the church
> I would set them apart;[2]

but to this thought in his Gospel of Beauty:

> The children now growing up should, if led by the spirit, wander over the whole nation in search of the secret of democratic beauty with their hearts at the same time filled to overflowing with the righteousness of God. Then they should come back to their own hearth and neighborhood and gather a little circle of their own sort of workers about them and strive to make the neighborhood and home more beautiful and democratic and holy with their special art . . . They should labor in their little circle expecting neither reward nor honors.

His simplicity of heart kept in hallowed trust that same tender, earnest, and sacred enthusiasm for beauty that set aflame his adolescent heart, so that in later years he could maintain this youthful ecstasy:

> Their reasons for living should be that joy in beauty which no wounds can take away, and that joy in the love of God which no crucifixion can end.

That joy was his eternally as he preached his gospel in his Church of Beauty. Limited by no bounds in his freedom of rapture, he called it the "Church of the Open Sky," and taught as his doctrine the joy of living with Love and Beauty, the joy of redemption, and the joy of the resurrection. These brought to him

> . . . throb of the mystic wings
> When the dove of God comes down
> And beats round my heart and sings.[3]

As he kneels beneath the moon, "With hills for my altar stairs," he sees his way to God

> . . . more dear
> Than love or life or youth,
>
> The road, it is the road,
> Mystical, endless, kind,
> Mother of visions vast,
> Mother of soul and mind.[4]

An idealist, he sang on his mendicant tours through the West a triad that foreshadows the Springfield of his vision and the hope of all America to be.

"The Proud Farmer" praises the man who made the land of his strength, who, in his integrity, bowed to none, but who respected all, the man to whom

> The farm and house of God . . . were one.

Next he takes his readers to the little prairie towns, symbols of white beauty that "calls for valiant song." In those "clean prairie lands" one cannot pass at night a village church "Without a touch of spirit-power." Nor can one pass the village school without the secret hope that some child-heart may be inspired in the future

> To make the whole wide village gleam
> A strangely carved celestial gem,
> Eternal in its beauty-light,
> The Artist's town of Bethlehem![5]

Closing this poem, Lindsay urges Springfield to stay small, lest it lose its ideals; he urges each child to keep his hopes perpetually as he should his religion; every

street to remain an aisle in the Church of Beauty; every
citizen to be generous to God, thus not letting greed
stain his heart. He begs Springfield to "Let Christ, the
beggar, teach divinity." Otherwise, he threatens

> I only know, unless her faith be high,
> The soul of this our Nineveh is doomed,
> Our little Babylon will surely die.[6]

Yet the Springfield of his vision, in the fullness of time,
will have been so swept by the tradition of beauty and
sublimity

> When men and maidens give fair hearts to Christ
> And white streets flame in righteous peace at last,[7]

that on earth Mary will be found in prototype again;
for Springfield will be

> Like Mary the manger queen
> Bringing the God of Light
> Till Christmas is here indeed
> And earth has no more night.[8]

For guidance along his own spiritual way and for grace
to strengthen his soul as he sang his gospel of rapture to
others, he literally renewed his vows yearly in the Catholic church of Springfield,

> . . . and this chief vow—
> To seek each year this shrine of deathless power,
> Keeping my spring-time cornland thoughts in flower,
> While labor-gnarled gray Christians round me bow.
>
> Arm me against great towns, strong spirits old!
> St. Francis keep me road-worn, music-fed,
> Help me to look upon the poorhouse bed
> As a most fitting death, more dear than gold.[9]

He begs help also to seek for company the sturdy pioneer

folk of his boyhood, and for further protection he cherishes a devotion to Mary. Indeed, from the Immaculate Queen and Patroness of the Church wherein he makes his vows, he implores this chastening:

> Scourge me, a slave that brings unhallowed praise
> To you, stern Virgin in this church so sweet,
> If I desert the ways wherein my feet
> Were set by Heaven, in my prenatal days.[10]

To that Queen of Virgins, he lifts his heart often in aspiration crying "Sweet Mary, make me clean. . . ." In the crusade against white slavery, he invokes her as the Mediatrix to free the bound. He prays, the rose-crowned lady from heaven in "Galahad, Knight Who Perished":

> . . . give us thy grace,
> Help us the intricate, desperate battle to face,
> Till the leer of the trader is seen nevermore in the land,
> Till we bring every maid of the age to one sheltering hand.

As a symbol of the true peace men seek, Lindsay gives a rose, for "The rose is Mary's heart." He says, too, that in the Catholic Church, Mary, as Star of the Sea, waits for the contrite of heart.

Of his interest in Catholicism, Mrs. Lindsay wrote:

> When he travels, which is a great deal of the time, he finds himself invariably seeking the open door and altar light of your Church, as do many, I think, who have not yet found the way home.

Again,

> As an art student in New York, Mr. Lindsay, though not a member of the church, spent much time in the Paulist Fathers Church—and such verses as 'Look You, I'll Go Pray' and others grew directly out of that.

To quote the poem:

> Look you, I'll go pray
> My shame is crying,
> My soul is gray and faint,
> My faith is dying . . .

From this devotional practice, he may have feared loss of Faith growing. "At Mass" confesses

> No doubt tomorrow I will hide
> My face from you, my King;

but prays for the present:

> Fill thou my soul with hidden wine
> To make this white hour great,

Then he glows with mystical rapture with his exquisite "Heart of God":

> O great heart of God,
> Once vague and lost to me,
> Why do I throb with your throb tonight,
> In this land, eternity?

Christ's rebirth in men's hearts and their consequent rights as members of His Mystical Body he takes as the Love needful the better to understand our fellowmen. All must stir from the sloth of paralyzing doubts, must give up selfish pride, guided by the star that leads

> Where dreaming ears the angel song shall win,
> Our Christmas shall be rare at dawning there,
> And each shall find his brother fair, . . .
> And hearts of earth shall find new birth
> And wake, no more to sin . . .[11]

Total trust in God as the First Cause of all Existence and recognition of redemption through Christ, he calls Springfield and the whole world to remember. Sure of

Christ's superior vision over that of Mohammed or Kali, Lindsay exults:

> This is our faith tremendous,
> Our wild hope, who shall scorn,
> That in the name of Jesus,
> The World shall be reborn![12]

His missionary enthusiasm to make mankind *ter quaterque beatus* he rapturously sings in a litany asking the great souls of history to pour their magnanimity upon men now. Though some leaders misled their age, Lindsay finds in each an influence to ennoble. Amenophis the Fourth, Moses, Siddartha, Phidias, Alexander, St. Paul, Augustine, Mohammed, Dante, Columbus, Titian, Shakespeare, Milton, Darwin, Lincoln, Emerson, Roosevelt, and Wilson he invokes for kindred spirit. Especially significant is his chant for Francis:

> Would I might wake St. Francis in you all,
> Brother of birds and trees, God's Troubadour,
> Blinded with weeping for the sad and poor.
> God make each soul the lonely leper's slave;
> God make us saints, and brave.[13]

Quickened by Franciscan joy, Lindsay grew rapturous over the Little Poor Man. Telling us he shares him in vision, at the time when the whole world cried, "War, war!" Lindsay heard the saint pray, "Peace, peace." As the patron of the city of San Francisco, the saint seems cowling his face as "He thinks of *gold . . . gold*." Then from the Yosemite valley the poet hears the prayers of the young, and, by virtue of penance, he sees their souls made white, "the opposite of gold."

Lindsay loved the child heart much as Francis did. With a child's rapture he made rhymes for little hearts,

the simplest in God's creations. Thinking of the sun saying its prayers for strength to ascend to the sky, he says,

> He leans on invisible angels,
> And Faith is his prop and his rod.
> The sky is his crystal cathedral,
> And dawn is his altar to God.[14]

Lindsay calls the full moon "the shield of faith," and the
dandelion, "My priest so gray and wise." He sings of the
clown and the angel, of Mab's book of Judgment, and of
the little shallop in which he sailed until he came "to
Zion, The gravel paths of God." For a little girl who
danced for him and whose feet glide to the whisper of
angels, he writes,

> I know a dancer who finds the true Godhead,
> Who lifts us toward peace.[15]

Gaily, joyously in children, sunshine, and Christmas
trees, Lindsay can find enchantment, thinking that at
least in heaven—

> You and I will be dancing.

> We will ride in the joy of God
> On circus horses white.[16]

There also will he give her great harps to play which
she can not refuse, "Or angels will mock . . . and turn
away." In the rapture of triumphal thought, her golden
head seems bent above his song and so transports him
to "The gorgeous treasure-pits of Heaven—Where angel
misers slake desire."

Reforming zeal moves Lindsay and burns him to spend
himself in reforms for the Anti-Saloon League of Illinois.
As a field-preacher in the campaign, he must have sur-

prised his listeners almost as much as we who read his cry

> King Arthur's men have come again,
> They challenge everywhere
> The foes of Christ's Eternal Church.[17]

With equal rapture he urges the campaigners on in the fight for conversion to the confidence of this closing cadence,

> Our God establishes his arm
> And makes the battle sure!

Then tired of the noise of the battle, realizing that the thunder can rage without him, he loses for a moment his zeal and turns to the reading of Khayyam with its lure of wine, flowers, and cup-bearers. Yet the zeal of his purpose conquers and he again drinks of the wine of God and resumes reforms.

Inflamed also by the evils of war Lindsay hurls a curse on kings who plunged the world in slaughter and declares that there are "no angel-flags in all the rag-array." St. Francis, Buddha, Tolstoi, St. John, and even Christ Himself could not convince these kings of wrong. Ecstatically stirred, Lindsay calls war the sin against the Holy Ghost. But his vision brings him assurance that Love of Christ will arouse pity among Mankind and finally move to a world peace.

Lindsay the Crusader for all manner of reforms is Lindsay the Revivalist. He uses the Negro in his primitive Congo setting to reveal their irrepressible high spirits, especially in the throes of religious conversion. Exhorting them to be washed in the Blood of the Lamb, Lindsay pictures, by noisy rhythms, violent imagery, and sudden climactic changes in mood, the savagery of the black in "getting religion." He reports this Negro sermon on Simon Legree:

> He beat poor Uncle Tom to death
> Who prayed for Legree with his last breath.
> Then Uncle Tom to Eva flew,
> To the high sanctoriums bright and new;
> And Simon Legree stared up beneath,
> And cracked his heels, and ground his teeth:
> And went down to the Devil.
>
> Simon Legree he reached the place,
> He saw one half of the human race,
> He saw the Devil on a wide green throne,
> Gnawing the meat from a big ham bone.
>
> And he said to Mister Devil:
>
> 'I see you drink your poison wine—
> Blood and burning turpentine.'
>
> And the Devil said to Simon Legree:
>
> 'I like your style so wicked and free,
> Come sit and share my throne with me.'
>
> And there they sit and gnash their teeth,
> And each one wears a hop-vine wreath.
> They are matching pennies and shooting craps,
> They are playing poker and taking naps.
> And old Legree is fat and fine:
> He eats the fire, he drinks the wine—
>   Down, down with the Devil;
>   Down, down with the Devil;
>   Down, down with the Devil.[18]

Similar grotesqueness marks the rapture with which Lindsay ushers General Booth into heaven. Having spent some nights among the "submerged tenth of the popu-

lation," as Booth called those who sought refuge in his
Salvation Army, Lindsay catches the spirit of the General.
Lindsay thrilled to the redeeming spirit that moved many
from the down-and-outers to be restored to goodness. After
a desperate struggle with these degraded charges, "Booth
died blind, yet still by faith he trod, Eyes still dazzled
by the ways of God." Booth's influence led his band to
Christ, Who made whole the afflicted. All were transformed by salvation. But, for Booth himself, Christ came
with a crown. And then "He saw King Jesus, They were
face to face."

Throughout the poem Lindsay is the zealot rejoicing
in the privilege of Redemption through Christ. Lindsay
beats his vision out loud on the big bass drum of a Salvation Army revival. For him "the poem grew out of a
triumph over despair and adversity."

But a more still mood came: "I heard Immanuel Singing" in a "millennial vision, really a vision," in which
Lindsay seemed to hear the Master singing

> Within his own good lands.

> His wounds were altogether healed.
> Old things had passed away.

Deep in Lindsay is his joy in the vision of the Resurrection. Meditation on death renews hope in his soul.
Then he feels that all eternity will he be united with the
one from whom he is parted. He says he thinks of Heaven
for

> . . . when man's dearest dies, 'tis then he goes
> To that old balm that heals the centuries woes,
> Then Christ's wild cry in all the street is rife:—
> 'I am the Resurrection and the Life.'[19]

Needing assurance that he will find the soul of that loved
one, he prays for a seraph-guide to help him "thread the
throng" on Judgment Day.

Vague and intangible as to the tenets of his belief in
the search for God; seemingly discordant at times, yet
always harmonized to the key of the theme, Lindsay
chants the gospel of need for rapture in every soul.
Touched by spiritual force from varying sects in his spiritual wandering Lindsay would, through his gospel of
Man's need for Beauty and rapture, change the grayness
of men's souls to a shining and white splendor. Whether
as in "Johnny Appleseed's Hymn to the Sun" in which
he prays for its innermost life, he harks back to the Garden
of Paradise; whether he awakens Springfield to righteous-
ness; or ushers Booth into Heaven; or shouts religion in
the Congo; Lindsay is aflame with rapture that dares Mankind to give up all before the challenge of Christ's love
for Man:

> Who can surrender to Christ? Where is the man so tran-
> scendent,
> So heated with love of his kind, so filled with the spirit
> resplendent
> That all of the hours of his day his song is thrilling and
> tender,
> And all of his thoughts to our white cause of peace
> Surrender, surrender, surrender?[20]

ROBERT P. T. COFFIN

Finds faith in the flash of a heron's wing

Dear Sister Mary James:

In reply to your query concerning my religious attitude, I can only wish it had fallen to my lot to possess the faith Thomas S. Jones, Jr., had. I have a kind of one, but not the one that enables me to see the Everlasting in the jewel-like faces of the men of his sonnets. He had the eyes of the eagles and of the old Saints of the church. I wish I had eyes like his. It isn't because I am not of the older Church—Tom wasn't either—for the seeing eyes can exist in unexpected places. But it is just that I can see manifestations of the good only in beautiful sudden flashes now and then, and not a complete vision, ever.

I can say this, though, that whenever I have found the footprints of great beauty, or of something of great and lovely strength, I have found the footprints of God. I am as sure of that as I am sure that cool water is good, or that hawks have beautiful wings. I have tried to say this in many, many poems—in my Golden Falcon, *and in many of the poems in my book,* The Yoke of Thunder. *So I feel sure that all splendid things, and all the strong, are* Religion, *and prove God. They are all separate manifestations that point to a beneficent power in behind the stars. The power which pushes up the daisies in a meadow is the same that sprinkles the daisies of the nebulae along the farthest reaches of space. I have said this in* Country Church, Now in the Hive, The Housing of the Lambs, *and especially in what I regard as my finest poem,* The Secret Heart. *In fact, now that I come to enumerate them, I find I have been trying to say this thing in ever so many of my poems of late years.*

I have never attempted, in prose or verse, to define Re-

May 7th. 1934

Dear Sister Mary Janes:

In reply to your query concerning my religious attitude, I can only wish it had fallen to my lot to possess the faith Thomas S. Jones, Jr., had. I have a kind of one, but not the one that enables me to see the Everlasting in the jewel-like faces of the men of his sonnets. He had the eyes of the eagles and of the old Saints of the church. I wish I had eyes like his. It isn't because I am not of the older Church— Tom wasn't, either— for the seeing eyes can exist in unexpected places. But it is just that I can see manifestations of the Good only in beautiful sudden flashes now and then, and not a complete vision, ever.

I can say this, though, that wherever I have found the footprints of great beauty, or of something of great and lovely strength, I have found the footprints of God. I am as sure of that as I am sure that cool water is good, or that hawks have beautiful wings. I have tried to say this in many, many poems — in my Golden Falcon, and in many of the poems in my book, The Voice of Thunder. So I feel sure that all splendid things, and all the strong, are Religion, and prove God. They are all separate manifestations that point to a beneficent power in behind the stars. The power which pushes up the daisies in a meadow is the same that sprinkles the daisies of the nebulae along the farthest reaches of space. I have said this in Country Church, now in the Hive, the Housing of the Lambs, and especially in what I regard as my finest poem, The Secret Heart. In fact, now that I come to enumerate them, I find I have been trying to say this thing in ever so many of my poems of late years.

I have never attempted, in prose or verse, to define Religion exactly. But in describing things that have moved me greatly, I have really, I think, been doing that. I guess, as you say, a man who is a poet could not do otherwise.

With every good wish for your undertaking,
Sincerely yours,
Robert P. Tristram Coffin

ligion exactly. But in describing things that have moved
me greatly, I have really, I think, been doing that. I guess,
as you say, a man who is a poet could not do otherwise.

With every good wish for your undertaking,

Sincerely yours,

(Signed) Robert P. Tristram Coffin

May 7, 1934.

NINE

FARM-BORN, Robert P. Tristram Coffin finds faith in the flash of a heron's wing; the vision has its setting in the country. To him

> . . . to know the country matters well
> Is to go with Dante into hell.
> It is a search for God, and dreary, lonely,
> A finding of stale marks of footprints only.[1]

And even more forcibly and comprehensively:

> . . . knowing country things four times of seven,
> Is all there still remains to term as heaven.[2]

But the vision is not an abiding one. As with Robinson, the search propels him on, while he believes in the existence of a Higher Divinity, truth comes but momentarily. But he is not content that it should do so, for, in speaking of the high religious faith of a contemporary poet, he makes this contrast:

> I wish it had fallen to my lot to possess something of the faith he had. I have a kind of one, but not the one that enables me to see the Everlasting in the jewel-like faces of the men of his sonnets. I wish I had eyes like his.

The beauty of a pastoral landscape, the simple joys and homely duties of country living, all the details of the woodlands symbolize religion to the poet. Accordingly, he sees manifestations of God in a heron's bill, in wings lifeless or broken, in the torn fur of a rabbit. Angels visit him in the blossoms of the overbearing fruit trees, and briars "have on every stem The color of the New Jerusalem." This idea he confirms in a letter:

> I can say this, that whenever I have found the footprints
> of beauty, or of something of great and lovely strength,
> I have found the footprints of God. I am as sure of that
> as I am sure that cool water is good, or that hawks have
> beautiful wings. I have tried to say this in many, many
> poems—in my *Golden Falcon* and in many poems in my
> book, *The Yoke of Thunder*. So I feel sure that all the
> lovely things, and all the strong are Religion, and prove
> God.

Each of these footprints of beauty, is, Mr. Coffin thinks,
a separate manifestation that points to the beneficent
power beyond the stars. It is the same power

> that pushes up the daisies in a country meadow and that
> sprinkles the daisies of the nebulae out along the farthest
> reaches of space.

All that he has written holds the flame-like brilliance
of his visions of Truth. But these visitants of beauty to
the poet are not always of the substance of earth's bright-
ness; they are of its doom as well. God, he tells us,

> . . . patterns blight and rust
> As carefully as skeins of nebulae
> Or blossoms in the eyeless midmost sea.[3]

To him, the sparrow snipping off the wings of the moth,
the larger fish devouring the smaller ones as they in turn
feed upon the amoeba, the sunbeam and the seed, the
wheat and the chaff, the apple and the worm struggling
for existence, all conform to the Creator's pattern for the
universe: death and birth wherein

> . . . each must give
> The death stroke and receive it, and so live.[4]

This realization of life as a pageant in which the pursued
and the pursuer, the captor and the captive, the destroyer

and the builder play the protagonist is a power working in Coffin's heart as he goes upon his quest. It finds expression in the lines:

> Life and death upon one tether
> And running beautiful together;[5]

> Important as the stars that must devour
> Their own fierce hearts to feed the lamps of love;[6]

> Nothing that men love the best
> At its flowering may rest;[7]

> Life and death before him played.[8]

On this same theme he reaches sublimity in

> You Ram who shape the universe
> And Lord who bleed to death
> Your hunger is our being fed,
> Your dying is our breath.[9]

The thought is purely Catholic, despite the poet's rejection of revealed religion and of a visible teaching Church. In his quest for truth, sense perception furnishes the sole data of knowledge. This follows logically from an admission made elsewhere; about the poem "The Housing of the Lambs," Coffin writes:

> It contains, I feel, the best definition of God, I have yet found, by my own means,

a happier mode of declaring that he takes exception to what God taught. The poem celebrates the reactions of a little girl, who, upon hearing the tender desolate cry in the night of the new-born, realizes that

> The thing her parents were about
> Out there where the embers were
> Was something sad and beautiful
> That had to do with God and her.

Mr. Coffin is emphatic in his belief in the existence of God as "The Startled Heron" reveals. He sings the ecstasy of coming suddenly upon the bird as it stood in the dawn, unconscious of any human existence, before winging splendid flight:

> Blue light on blue sky, he shot,
> Something more complete than thought.
>
> Grace created at a bound,
> A burning bush without a sound.
>
> Up and gone an instant's space,
> Godhead passes before my face.

In something as unpoetic as a barnacle he recognizes that

> . . . there is some fierce intelligence
> Beyond these creatures that are hand entire;[10]

Even the cold beauty of a jelly-fish inspires him to nobility of thought:

> The power that throws up the surf
>   Of stars unborn on outer space
> Shows as surely in this veined
>   Creature which is opal lace.[11]

Nevertheless, he is concerned principally with God as the Creator. So universal does he find the art of God that he is led to chant "The Maker," a Genesis in summary:

> I know the Maker moves in paradox.
> He spends his equal pains on mouse and ox,
>   Stiff flowers of the crystal, sudden vines
>   Of lightning.

.   .   .   .   .

He shapes the single stars of cockerels' eyes,
The nest of crystal mirrors for the flies.
He forges granite, and he spreads the bloom
On the bat-wings velvet in the gloom.

In order with this attribute of Omnipotence, he celebrates directly or indirectly the Hand of God. In the life-
history of a bee, an unseen hand moves, fashions, weaves,
and then leaves

> . . . a loveliness like a star.

> And this same hand at this same hour
> Bends far fire to its power.

> Sets the bees of fire free
> Which are the singing nebulae.[12]

And when the bees pursue their systematic course among
the flowers, he would impress that it

> . . . was drawn by One
> Who made an archer of the wilful sun

> And broke the comets on his brazen wheel
> To run his errands with a blazing heel.[13]

The same Hand "sowed the universe with seed," "set the
sea in place," and for the fireflies "forged the first thin
crystal of an eye."

That Robert P. Tristram Coffin seems to believe in
Divine Providence is a logical sequence to his faith in
God as the Author of the Universe. Love and protection
characterize the interest in one's own handwork. The love
that the poet feels is infinite; he says that it is deeper
than the roots of trees and older than any love he knows
either this day or tomorrow. It is

> The love that holds the thunder and the sea
> In the hollow of its palm and charts
>   The voyage of death through mayflies' emerald hearts
>   Forever and forever.[14]

It guards and guides those sailors of the air, the wild geese which travel instinctively through danger into safety. For consistently with the idea of an intelligent Creator,

> It could not be there was no goal,
> No plan to pattern, not a soul
> Sitting calm somewhere above
> With palms above some lamp of love
>   And planning new and keener things
>   When these exquisite pairs of wings,
> Built so clean and long and right,
> Helped one another in their flight.[15]

God, furthermore, feeds the lonely birds. Wherefore the poet is confident that eventually he will stand

> In between the wings
> Of the great and last white clouds . . .
> Shoulder there to shoulder with them . . .[16]

and rest his burning face "in the white, sweet curve of His hand."

Once he is led to question God's care of humanity, but immediately hope insures a comfort:

> If there is not as yet designed
> A god to love our human kind,
>
> I feel sure one will arise
> From our hopes and seize the skies,
>
> Grasp its mighty lamps and keep
> Watch upon us when we sleep.[17]

God's eternal vigilance of man he centers in the symbol of an open eye. It watches "hot and steady there, like a spider in its snare." Unwavering love and anxiety, untiring and unmitigated zeal it lavishes upon us.

> He will not, will not trust us from his eye.
> His eyes are everywhere; we must not dream
>   That he is of our image; his eyes gleam
>   In flaming rows around his jealous head.
> They see in every corner.[18]

Yet, in sequel, he can write this perplexity concerning an antlered head that fixed staring, sightless eyes on him in youth and unduly aggravated his fears:

> And who knows but the great, mysterious shape
>   We feel has eyes on all the things we do,
> Between the cradle and the grave, is such
>   Another sightless head, if we but knew?[19]

Robert P. T. Coffin thus affirms his belief in a Supreme and Infinite Personal Being to whom man owes worship. Poems like "The Grindstone," "Ways to Look at Stars," and "Anemones" hold his affirmations:

> Out of this wheel the splendid words of God
> Ran like sparks and cried themselves abroad;

> A son of God, then crucified, forgotten;

> The pith of us is silent as the trees
> And worshipful as bowed anemones.

The Divinity of his belief is, therefore, apart from the universe. Twice however, he is self-refuting. "In this frail transparency" of a jelly-fish, "God moves essentially and wholly." Is not this Pantheism? "The Heron" seems to indicate the same idea:

> I know God finds night lovelier
>   Than day, for all its light
> For I have seen a heron go
>   Dreaming across the night.[20]

Elsewhere he is not at variance in his quest for truth. He rises to the mystical in "Tower of Silence" on the symbolism of a lighthouse in his native Maine:

> And when a man is master of a light
> That he can send out like a silver rod
> Between a life and death, he ought to know
> Something of the joy of being God.

Equally exultant is his "Song for March." The beauty of light more brilliant than the whiteness of swans and of color radiating from "jet and amber, sleet and shine" raises him to the mystical interpretation of God's treasure box being broken and transforming all the world with opalescent splendor:

> The box of God is broken now,
> And all the world runs pearls.[21]

That Mr. Coffin has complete faith in objects of sense perception revealing God to him, we have had his own words as evidence. "Saint Brandan of the West" is further declaration:

> To be a fever of joy that burns around the earth
> Like the stars which follow day in everlasting mirth,
>   To lie below the sail,
>   My crystal vase of winds—
> *This* were wife and child, brother and church to me.

There in the vast expanse of sea, a cathedral of nature, Robert P. Tristram Coffin could glimpse God as he did in the passing heron. Again his faith would warrant only the sudden flash of truth. Yet desire would not be wanting in his heart, but only the privilege of accepting truth in the light of revelation. But for that he offers his quest as an "Apologia" when he writes:

> I was born too late to lean
> On the arms that are unseen.

BOOK THREE: POETS NATURALLY CHRISTIAN

T. S. ELIOT

Emerges from the waste land

Dear Sister:

In reply to your letter of December 1st, perhaps the simplest account that I can give is to say that I was brought up as a Unitarian of the New England variety; that for many years I was without any definite religious faith, or without any at all; that in 1927 I was baptised and confirmed into the Church of England; and that I am associated with what is called the Catholic movement in that Church, as represented by Viscount Halifax and the English Church Union. I accordingly believe in the Creeds, the invocation of the Blessed Virgin and the Saints, the Sacrament of Penance, etc.

Yours faithfully,

(Signed) T. S. Eliot

6 December 1932.

T. S. ELIOT
B-11 ELIOT HOUSE
CAMBRIDGE

6 December 1932.

Sister Mary James,

    Couvent de Notre Dame,

        Fellsway East,

           Malden, Mass.

Dear Sister,

        In reply to your letter of December 1st, perhaps
the simplest account that I can give is to say that I was
brought up as a Unitarian of the New England variety; that for
many years I was without any definite religious faith, or
without any at all; that in 1927 I was baptised and confirmed
into the Church of England; and that I am associated with what
is called the Catholic movement in that Church, as represented
by Viscount Halifax and the English Church Union. I accordingly believe in the Creeds, the invocation of the Blessed Virgin and the Saints, the Sacrament of Penance etc.

                Yours faithfully,

                T. S. Eliot

TEN

T. S. ELIOT has emerged from *The Waste Land*. And from that region, sterile in belief, he has risen to the heights of Christian faith. Although he has said: ". . . for many years I was without any definite religious faith or without any at all," still his most arid period of soul strength was not a time of complete, spiritual drouth. Now and then he had tasted of the Living Water of Truth; there was an intuitive vision of the word which, in later verse, he was to celebrate with profound reverence. In those days of what he calls "unbelief," he says:

> We would see a sign!
> The word within a word, unable to speak a word,
> Swaddled with darkness. In the juvenescence of the year
> Came Christ the tiger.[1]

Of the Word Made Flesh he feels a haunting Presence. In the barrenness of *The Waste Land*, he sees a third companion, a figure that would recall the One who joined the two Disciples on their way to Emmaus. Is it the consciousness of the Invisible that quickens him to this poignant cry of soul?

> Burning burning burning burning
> O Lord Thou pluckest me out
> O Lord Thou pluckest
> burning[2]

Death's other kingdom, the kingdom not "of the hollow men" comes within his prospect of belief. In that thought is the Peace that surpasseth all understanding, as held in his equivalent verse: "Shantih shantih shantih." A knowledge of the Word, the existence of Permanent Being in a state of eternity and man's enjoyment thereof, together with a unity of Faith epitomize the creed of Mr. Eliot, it seems, before he accepted the teaching of any set system of organized religion.

For the period of his spiritual wayfaring, an act of atonement follows: symbolically he calls the transition *Ash Wednesday*. Having found the Way, the Truth, and the Life, for Mr. Eliot there will be no retrogression, no turning back, he says. Is he emphatic or wavering in this repetition?

> Because I do not hope to turn again
> Because I do not hope
> Because I do not hope to turn
> Desiring this man's gift and that man's scope . . .[3]

Soul progress will mean not only humble submission to, but resignation to the aspects of the present, not the resignation in which one surfeits because of the uncertainty of the actual, but the resignation in which one tempers desire because the actual rules the future in an instant. Thus in time most secure, glory may be insecure. Furthermore, time and space are always finite. The flowering of trees and the flowing of the spring are transitory; in them all is nothing. With these points of reflection, the poet, after a sense of complete exhaustion from the struggle of the waste land of doubt, rejoices in the acceptance of fact and prays that with the mercy he trusts God will grant him there will come the forgetfulness of the past with its deeds and its omissions. Wherefore he makes this lyric act of love:

> Let these words answer
> For what is done, not to be done again
> May the judgment not be too heavy upon us.[4]

Meanwhile, the conflict of the soul is constant and severe. Hope, the wings of the spirit, will be earth-bound, beating in vain the air in flight from the trivial. Though the will may aspire to rarer heights, yet there will come, he prays, that indifference known only to the seekers of perfection, the disposition to care and not to care, the desire to rest only in God's Will and in this saving plea:

> Pray for us sinners now and at the hour of our death
> Pray for us now and at the hour of our death.[5]

If *Ash Wednesday* is Mr. Eliot's atonement, it is his *Apologia* too. Soul-suffering, aggravated by the vision of threatening torments through the demon of doubt, but lessened by his escape from the occasion of these evils, is the inheritance of the poet as he mounts the triple stairway that leads to his inheritance. And as he enters the land of that inheritance: faith, as high as is humanly possible for man to reach by himself, faith that is "strength beyond hope and despair," we overhear him pray:

> Lord, I am not worthy
> Lord, I am not worthy
>   but speak the word only.[6]

As if in token, nature takes on the aspect of rejoicing. In procession, between the ranks of the old years of his life in harmonies of violet and varied green, or "fiddles and of flutes," there walk the years which are to be, the years of his rebirth. In "white and blue, in Mary's colour," they come, restoring

> One who moves in the time between sleep and waking,
>   wearing
> White light folded, sheathed about her folded,[7]

and singing a new canticle of love, the hope and the symbol of redemption.

As when the Word first spoken was unspoken, unheard by those who would not hear; those who, in the hardness or confusion of their hearts, could not hear the stillness of the word; those who heard but did not harken; the same Redeeming Word is spoken. Mr. Eliot has heard the Word. From the fullness of his heart he asks if the Spirit of Religion, to many veiled, will intercede for those who prefer the darkness to the light, those who in the midst of light are blinded by the light, those who rejoice in prosperity, but murmur in adversity, and those who, in a garden of grace, choose a desert of despair. For them from the fullness of his regenerated heart, he reëchoes, "O my people."

Reborn spiritually, T. S. Eliot rejoices in his redemption to grace and seals his act of atonement with his opening prayer of trust and confidence:

> Although I do not hope to turn again
> Although I do not hope
> Although I do not hope to turn
> Wavering between the profit and the loss
>
> .   .   .   .
> . . . the weak spirit quickens to rebel . . .[8]

and this exquisite tribute to that hovering spirit with which he desires consummate union:

> Blessed sister, holy mother, spirit of the fountain, spirit of
>   the garden,
> Suffer us not to mock ourselves with falsehood
>
> .   .   .   .
> Teach us to sit still
> Even among these rocks,
> Our peace in His will
> And even among these rocks
>
> .   .   .   .
> Suffer me not to be separated
> And let my cry come unto Thee.[9]

Ash Wednesday is Marian tribute also. In the land where "neither division nor unity matters," bones, scattered at the final dissolution, exult with whitened splendor in the presence of that virtue which is Marylikeness. Before the virginal, they exalt the Single, the Mystical Rose with these lyric lines:

> End of the endless
> Journey to no end
> Conclusion of all that
> Is inconclusible
> Speech without word and
> Word of no speech
> Grace to the Mother
> For the Garden
> Where all love ends.[10]

Praise of the Mother, they are Eliot's faith in the Son, in man's resurrection, and in the many mansions beyond. Each of these doctrines T. S. Eliot professes to believe. Note his own words:

> . . . in 1927 I was baptized and confirmed into the Church of England; and I am associated with what is called the Catholic movement in that Church, . . . I accordingly believe in the Creeds, the invocation of the Blessed Virgin and the Saints, the Sacrament of Penance, etc.

The Journey of the Magi, as told by one of the Wise Men, may perhaps be accepted as allegorical. The attendant circumstances of traveling at that time of year: cold and inconvenience, inhospitality and delay, doubt and ignorance, contrast with the hope which their spirit yearned to find in the Birth. But it was a Birth unified with Death. It revealed to them a death and yet it gave the vision of life, a new life for them in this world. The Birth they saw was as bitter as their own death which they had experienced spiritually, when they willingly and sadly renounced their most intimate beliefs. Withal, they rejoiced in their rebirth, their reception into the new dispensation; and Mr. Eliot, for another regeneration of spirit, would welcome similar death. He says:

> . . . this Birth was
> Hard and bitter agony for us, like Death, our death.
> We returned to our places, these Kingdoms,
> But no longer at ease here, in the old dispensation,
> With an alien people clutching their gods.
> I should be glad of another death.[11]

A Song for Simeon is further consolation from the Word, "the Infant, the still unspeaking and unspoken Word." Again in Birth there is the revelation of death. This time it is the aged Simeon who sees salvation. It is his "Nunc dimittis": he sings,

> Grant me thy peace.
>
> .   .   .   .
>
> I am tired with my own life and the lives of those after me,
> I am dying in my own death and the deaths of those after me.
> Let thy servant depart,
> Having seen thy salvation.[12]

Having emerged from *The Waste Land* and found the Pearl of Great Price, T. S. Eliot has carefully preserved his treasure, guarding it safely on the heights of reflection and prayer. He seems to see life now in terms of souls, and in *Animula* he traces lovingly the story of a little soul. "Issues from the hand of God," he says, "the simple soul." There is no mistaking here the direct creation by God of man's immortal soul and its subservience to its surroundings in childhood until the growing years disturb with the perplexity of "is and seems," of "may and may not," of appetite and will. Then comes the pain of sense to separate fact and fancy: the wonder that curls

> . . . up the small soul in the window seat
> Behind the Encyclopaedia Britannica.[13]

Experience, the willing pupil but the stern teacher, weakens the will, misshapes the body, and destroys the taste. And the soul, simple and Christian by nature, lives then only "in the silence of the viaticum." Bringing his listeners through the life history of any little soul, Mr. Eliot does not leave it victimized to sin and death; he commends it to the prayers of his listeners. Now he asks prayers for the over-ambitious, the greedy, now for the one strayed from the fold, and now for those whose death was untimely, but always for each one of us "now and at the hour of our birth."

The Rock holds Mr. Eliot's faith with firm security. Associated with the Catholic movement of the Church of England, as represented by Viscount Halifax and the English Church Union, the poet writes the pageant as the summation of his belief: implicit faith in the teachings of that Church which he would have continuous with the Church of pre-Reformation days as the solution of all worldly problems.

The play deals with the actual building of a church. Over its construction the canaille dispute, for in their perverseness they deny not only the existence, but the necessity of a God. Consequently, they question any form or frame of worship of Divinity. But for these rebel forces there is always a counter-force. Such a saving force is the "Rock"; through it the poet stresses his credo: "A Church for us all and work for us all even unto this last."

Living not in the past or in the future, but taking care

for the present only, the Rock counsels; sowing the seed, not reaping the harvest; universal not particular charity:

> The desert is not only around the corner,
> The desert is squeezed in the tube-train next to you,
>
> . . . .
>
> The desert is in the heart of your brother.

Yet, to the laborers who await but a dividend, there is no conviction of making perfect their will or of building what is good, as the poet says. Only when they see with the seeing eye will they believe. They witness, therefore, the past in the person of Mellitus, who preaching Christianity to Anglo-Saxon England converted a king and his subjects. Realizing, then, that worldliness and sin have created all the problems of humanity and that the Church alone can solve them, the workmen start the building, but on marshy land. Again, a voice from the past must inspire faith in God for their perseverance. Here a monk of the time of Henry makes clear a necessity: faith that the angels and saints may invoke God's blessing on their endeavors, while the chorus rebukes men for perverting God's blessings to foolish purpose. Much have they read, but the reading was not of God; much have they built, but not with Him. And this for a warning portentous:

> A colony of cavies or a horde of active marmots
> Build better than they that build without the Lord.
>
> . . . .
>
> Where there is no temple there shall be no homes.

Forces of evil from without, those to which the Scriptures bear witness, assail the building in progress. Agitation, as known in the present from communism and militarism, revives, for the obstinate and the doubting, scenes of foreign invasion that show yet again that the Church is built upon the firm foundation of rock, that it will fulfil its Divine mission of prevailing against the gates of hell. Always in the lapse of time Christ will be crucified; always will there be sacrificial victims. And for double assurance to the builders, the chorus adds:

> And if blood of Martyrs is to flow on the steps
> We must first build the steps;
> And if the Temple is to be cast down
> We must first build the Temple.

Between doubt and fear the workmen and even the Chorus weakens, to receive again hope from the past. The crusades in vision strengthen; the Church works not alone but under a guiding spirit. And in the abiding of that Divine Spirit man must believe now as he did when Peter the Hermit called:

> Remember the faith that took men from home
> At the call of a wandering preacher.
> Our age is an age of moderate virtue
> And of moderate vice
> When men will not lay down the Cross
> Because they will never assume it.
> Yet nothing is impossible, nothing,
> To men of faith and conviction.
> Let us therefore make perfect our will.
> O God, help us.

Once more hope and wisdom strengthen and the workmen proceed with the Church for the one and all, to be interrupted only by criticism decrying the externals of the building which would suggest the excesses of Reformation times when, more to fill coffers than promote art, simplicity was a canon. However, artisans of all ranks contribute to the glory of the temple, and as symbolic of Heaven's favor the Chorus moves to this praise:

Lord, shall we not bring these gifts to Your service?

. . . .

For life, for dignity, grace and order,

. . . .

The formed stone, the visible crucifix,
The dressed altar, the lifting light,
Light
Light
The visible reminder of Invisible Light.

A mighty "Te Deum" swells to grand crescendo when the "Rock, now St. Peter," interprets the Temple, not the Visible Church which earth knows as the work of the Word, but the Temple that is God to Whose Image all the blessed in Heaven are transformed. And there

. . . is night no more, but only
Light
Light
Light of the Light.

It is in the light of faith, in that Light that T. S. Eliot stands as he looks from the heights on the "Church for us all and work for us all and God's World for us all even unto this last."

ALFRED NOYES:

Balladist and oarsman of God

ELEVEN

*T*HE UNKNOWN GOD is the *Apologia* of Alfred
Noyes, mapping the course over which he cut his
way to Truth. The dangerous waters of agnosticism led,
rather than misled, him in his spiritual voyaging. As Noyes
went on in Darwin's reasoning and that of Spencer, Haeckel, and Huxley, he found that the "Absolute" was "God."
What seemed suprarational to the agnostic was supernatural to Noyes. That vision he reached through his insight,
namely, grace and his office as poet:

> I had never heard of the ontological proof of the existence
> of God; and yet, after wading through endless pages of
> discursive reasoning in later life, it seems to me that all
> the essentials were mine by intuition, or direct mental
> vision, as far back as I can remember.[1]

In verse he says,

> Mist in the valley, yet I saw,
> And in my soul I knew
> The gleaming City whence I draw
> The strength that then I drew . . .[2]

Other points of orthodoxy he infers as having come
from no studied system of thought. So spontaneous were
they that they expressed themselves in verse. For definite
purpose, he cites the essence of the Epistle to the Ephe-
sians which he early comprehended in the physical law
of water seeking its own level. This he sang in the "Sacred
Oak." In the words of the disciple:

> Now that he ascended, what is it, but because he also
> first descended into the lower parts of the earth? He that
> descended is the same that ascended above all the heavens
> in order that he might fill all things;[3]

Noyes interprets it thus:

> . . . Still He descends
> From heaven. The increasing worlds are still
> His throne.
> And His creative Calvary and His tomb
> Through which He sinks, dies, triumphs with each and all,
> And ascends multitudinous and at one
> With all the hosts of His evolving doom.
> His vast redeeming strife,
> His everlasting life,
> His love, beyond which not one bird, one leaf can fall.[4]

As the oarsman of God bending towards that sheltering harbor of Love, Alfred Noyes works out his intuitive belief in a Divine Intelligence as opposed to the scientific theory of his time. And for Britannia, his consuming devotion, he pleads repeatedly as in "Nelson's Year" and "In Time of War" that she resist the surgings of doubt and misbelief that would swamp her or turn her from the course toward that port of Wisdom which would draw all things to Itself.

> Cleave the clouds of doubt asunder,
> And speed the union of mankind in one divine desire.

> England, God help thee, let no jot or tittle
> Of Love's last law go past thee without heed.

The Law of Love drew Noyes unto Itself. His was a soul naturally Christian. Intellectually he played for awhile with "blind chance" and questioned the "triumph of man." Emotionally he renewed his heart with that cry that outlasts Time, "Before the world was God!" England's watchword of the sea. Yet despite his willing faith, he wondered on life as a mystery. Is life more than a mere scheme for testing man's endurance in suffering, giving him thereby knowledge for living more worthily here only to lose it? Nineteenth century logic taught annihilation. This from "The Open Door":

> . . . earth and all its race
> Must pass and leave no trace
> On that blind sky.

But that was only another hypothesis. Must this theory loaded with the pessimism of Arnold and Huxley necessarily clear up the issue? Might not living in time point to living in eternity? Might not the wings of strife rise to the splendor of glory? Here was an "open door." Reason kept it open for the poet. Faith permitted him to enter through this hope. Hopefully he sings, mine is

> . . . the creed
> That leaves for God, indeed,
>   For God, and man,
> One open door whereby
> To prove His world no lie
> And crown His plan.[5]

In the early poems by Noyes is open profession of faith in this dogma. In starlight on a stormy sea, in the moan of the wind, the murmur of the trees, and the flow of tears, Noyes hears the "Loom of the Weaver." The hound, the fawn, the dove, the fern, and the rose "are all one woof of the weaving," and, like them, are we for "the one warp threads us through." His realization of our oneness with creation he impresses even through the play of the rhythm to which all nature moves in harmony. A child swings on a gate, sunflowers nod, winds blow, tides rise and fall, planets roll

> . . . to my cracked old tune,
> Hey! diddle, diddle, the cat and the fiddle,
> the cow jumped over the moon.[6]

Noyes felt the Infinite Mind that fashioned a toadstool
worked to that cosmic tune of eternal rhythm.

But rhythm as a medium for the perception of a First
Cause is too far removed from common experience to be
generally accepted. A poet, however, makes such a theory
acceptable. Noyes takes unreflecting man back to the
primal earth; farther than primal slime, and still farther
to the reputed beginning, Blind Nothingness. In that
setting, he asks:

> Did this Nothingness give rise to your sublimest thought
>   and mine?
> Did it set an Olivet on the sky-line?
> Did it mould a praying child, "One woman's
> love-lit face,"[7] or "One martyr ringed with fire?"[8]

Then he dares this challenge:

> Will you have courage, then, to front that law
>   . . . That nothing can proceed—
> Not even thought, not even love—from less
>   Than its own nothingness?
>
> .   .   .   .   .
>
> Dare you rekindle, then,
>   One faith for faithless men,
> And say you found, on that dark road you trod,
>   *In the beginning—GOD?*[9]

Noyes finds the death of Francis Thompson an opportunity to sing the wonder of creation and the joy of vision.
To Thompson's child-heart, could not vision have been
almost perfect? It would mean a quest of the Nothingness, not of Nescience, but the Nothingness that "was and
was not," that chaste Nothingness that conceived Light
in Chaos and brought man out of the slime. Would not
that dreaming heart see the flora and the fauna in their
virgin beauty, and, at the innermost shrine, the chastest
of all its white symbols?

The world's Birth-mystery,
    Whereto the suns are shade?
Lo, the white breast divine—
    The holy Mother-maid.[10]

This vision would hold, likewise, the shadow of the Cross
with its Divine Victim. His Hands nail-pierced that His
Outstretched Arms might embrace the East and the West
and enrich with the drops of His Precious Blood the sin-
stained dust of earth.

Next Noyes sings a ballad of "Creation." At the genesis
of life when there was neither Time nor Space, God pro-
claiming Himself as the embodiment of all and declaring
His single existence, in the fullness of His Love made
a beautiful world. Into it He placed the beauty of the
seas, trees, flowers, grass, suns, moons, stars, rainbows, and
birds, all for a little child whose soul would be in his own
keeping. God saw in His Omniscience the fall of the child,
but still Noyes in his vision heard Him sing about man's
spiritual growth to be:

And when he is older he shall be
    My friend and walk here by My side;
Or—when he wills—grow young with Me,
    And, to that happy world where once we died
    . . . Buy life once more with our immortal breath,
    . . . And taste of Love and Death.

Miltonic, he introduces Deity again. Once more he
sounds the Mighty Voice: "I am that I am." It is the
Divine Paradox, the Changeless among the ever-changing,
the One Who is the Beginning and the End, the One Who
Knows neither life nor death, Who is neither good nor
evil, yet greater than either, Who to the mystic is the Dark
Night of the Soul and, withal, the Light of Life, His Love,
so comprehensive that it is the one circle whose centre

is everywhere and whose circumference is nowhere which
in "Paradox" Noyes defines thus:

> . . . the Sphere without circumference:
> I only and for ever comprehend
> All others that within me meet and blend.
>
> . . . I am the Lord . . .
> The wings of my measureless love go forth
> To cover you all: they are free as the wings of the wind.

Apparently atoning for transient doubt, Noyes publicly
breaks faith with scepticism. Tired of the pride of the
sophist, weary of loving argument for its own sake, of
theorizing instead of practising love, and that in the
abstract, Noyes goes back, so the sceptic would say, to
the infinite Love of the child who sees the God that transcends all fact. For those who may have increased his
doubt, he will wield

> . . . the flaming sword of nineteen hundred years,
> The sword of the High God's answer, *O Pilate, what is
> truth?*[11]

Amid their scoffs and jeers, he rejoices in the gift of faith,
seeing around him the deep peace of Christ's Love. Then
"Vicisti Galilaee!" comes as his grand confession as he
sees Calvary thus hourly renewed in souls that suffer and
are silent, and even in every wayside flower, He hears
that forsaken cry "Father, Father!" roll over life's tem-
pestuous seas as "The Sailor King" bends his oars through
dangerous waters barring his way to the haven-like vision
of the City Beyond:

> The beacon-fire of an Empire's soul;
>   The worth of that light—seamen know
> Through all the deaths that the storm can bring
>   The crown of their comrade—ship aglow
>   The signal-fire of the king.[12]

That safer harbor of Eternity engrosses the heart of Noyes. Naturally Christian, bending his course by the north star of Truth, he prays to live not long but wholly in conformity with the law of Love. Meditation on agonies borne for Love's Sake, Calvaries that have brought complete separation, move him to yearn for the cross that later chastens his spirit: death that has so tended its flowers for him that it has mingled earth with heaven in the sense of his loss. Can this be nineteenth-century pessimism? No. Rather it is joy born in the heart of a poet who can sing in "The War Widow":

> . . . There is no hope, no way,
> No truth, no life, but leads through Christmas Day.

This is the joy of the idealist;

> The joy that casts aside this earth
> For immortality.[13]

Rejoicing in this love, the poet recognizes happy cosmic signs about him. Eternity endlessly passes before him as the stars wheel above the ranks of the dead moving onward into the silences. In the faces of those moving "Away to eternity," he sees "Hints and facets of One—the Eternal." And in the sea he quickens to the cry of the weary-hearted whom Love will refresh. He sings in allegory the Resurrection: a soul who committed in its heart, against reason, all the indignities Love can receive, who denied Love supreme honor among His creatures as well as the symbols of all Power, reducing Love to mere energy generating matter, at length arises, with the Saviour, to the Miracle of Love and to this courageous faith:

> . . . We challenge heaven above
> Now, to deny our slight ephemeral breath
> Joy, anguish, and that everlasting love
> Which triumphs over death.[14]

With childlike joy delighting in the imaginative past, he turns back over the sea of fancy to an enchanted isle floating between earth and heaven. There he had passed from angelic birth to childhood as a boy in the Paradisal Land until a breath as strange as that which transplanted him to ether changed him into manhood and his enchanted isle into a tomb. From that tomb he will again emerge not on a sea of fancy, but on the waters of truth, when he will be reenchanted "In Paradise, in Paradise."

With sure childlike joy, Noyes looks to the ages that will bring the Eternal Spring. With wide-eyed wonder men will go to God Who will know all their questionings about their souls, now

> A temporal chalice of Eternity
> Purple with beating blood of the hallowed grape.[15]

Faith in eternity is his explanation of the justice of God. Promises like: *Fear not, I have overcome the world,* will not pass as an idle word. Love that protects the lily and the bird will be the unfailing friend to those who have made His Image their guiding star. Friendly in life, will He not be as friendly in death? "Compensation" assures and reassures:

> . . . What friend belies
> His love with idle breath?
>   We read it in each other's eyes,
> And ask no more in death.

Equity requires that the Master pay His debt to those whom He has made. Never will he put down life to matter. More convincingly the poet pleads that only when insensate matter shall efface the light in a child's eyes shall there be room for doubt. Then he speaks to the pessimists his final word of sure faith:

Never shall time subordinate . . .
The love in one child heart to this blind dust.
If that young faith within her eyes
Were noble, that which lies
Beyond the world is nobler. This I know.[16]

Agony in the World War kept the poet's eyes fixed on God as the Way, the Truth, and the Life in the struggle. Over the flags of the allied nations assembled from the East and the West, Noyes hears a chant, the "breath of God" intoning

. . . I am His Laughter.
I am His Liberty. That is my name . . .
Let there be light over all His creation.[17]

Over the warring troops Noyes sees a light that was the Cross of Christ. As in ages gone, this radiance lighted man on a path to peace: peace in the triumph of right and in the Hope of the Holy City. From its sacred wood those who manned the ships of war heard again the Voice: "I will make you then Fishers of men." Thereupon they prayed that God would bless them as they fought to shield the weak. But whether or not they live to conquer wrong on the field of battle, they will

Behind the veil of earth and sea and sky
. . . live and move and work with nobler powers.[18]

The trenches, to the unthinking man, are mere scenes of carnage, but Alfred Noyes, thinking of the Divine Commander, sees them in white beauty as hallowed warriors of a countless host soaring above with angelic guides.

Christmas 1919! At last Noyes demands true peace. But there is no peace, no peace in England now. Only through the mystic birth of Christ in men's hearts can men find lasting peace. Only thus is peace preserved through a perfect communion with Peace and Love. Noyes sings the tale of Michael Oaktree, who for eighty years walked in the Presence of God. His death was indeed a going home with God. Now Noyes perceives more fully

> . . . how many means
> Of grace there are for those that never lose
> Their sense of membership in this divine
> Body of God . . .
> There is one God, one Love, one everlasting
> Mystery of Incarnation. . . .[19]

He knows also that there is an everlasting Calvary, for he feels that agony when deed runs counter to desire. When for a paltry sum, an ignoble thought or deed, he sells the Master, he hears in his heart all the cries of Golgotha: "Behold, behold the man! Crucify!"

With equal faith he believes in help from the Holy Ghost. Abiding ever, It reveals Itself in the fragrance of the wild thyme, in the tang of the sea, in limpid water, in the "light on a face or touch of a hand." While men deny the Paraclete, yet It has comforted all. In witness of his faith in Abiding Love comes this poet's sacred invocation:

> Veni, Creator,
> Paraclete![20]

that the Comforter may spread shielding wings over him as It did in Bethlehem on the first Christmas night. In that "pure birth," the poet celebrates the virginity of Mary as he does again in "The Statue": A youth, prostrate before a shrine of earthly love, implores pity from its patron. But death takes his life for a boon and gives him vision lovelier than Aphrodite's classic glance:

. . . One more beautiful in the morning clouds,
The Mother of Bethlehem, to whom he prayed
Himself, but never knew her till that hour
So beautiful.

That Mother and her Child, Eternal Love, receives
fitting homage when Alfred Noyes, in a message to Har-
vard, tries to lead America and the world to follow the
Voice that says, "I am the Way, the Truth, the Life, the
Light." Since chaos it has sounded, persuading men to
the Law that makes glory, might, beauty, and mercy conform to the One Pattern. That Law, Noyes says, is the
only true Liberty and only in it shall "we find our own."
But Nations have refused to listen, have chosen in its stead
Barabbas, have made blind chance their choice. Agonies
from the Great War, too, have renewed for the poet the
passion of Calvary. Outrages against innocence have raised
another crucifixion whose "shadow veils the sun." Yet in
the darkness of this agony of war, Alfred Noyes sings
the Eternal Christ as the Way

Whereby we reach the peace which is not death
But the triumphant harmony of Life,
Eternal Life, immortal Love, the Peace
Of worlds that sing around the throne of God.[21]

CHARLES WILLIAMS

Sings the mystery of love

LETTER FROM CHARLES WILLIAMS

You ask me to state my belief. But since, philosophically, it is not possible for us to say that we know anything, any such statement must rest on a hypothesis. Some sort of hypothesis is necessary, certainly, in order that we may act at all. But only when we recognize one which, essentially, does not change, which becomes a first principle to our lives, can we choose to accept it as true, and elaborate from it a belief which accords with our experience. The hypothesis which I first willed to accept, and which life confirms in me, is the Christian one, briefly: the Deity of Love and the Incarnation of Love, and I therefore formally accept the three Creeds, and the Christian Faith (as declared in the rituals of the Church of England).

The Incarnation is the central event of our existence; an Act made inevitable by, and involved in, the first Creation. It is central to us in that it forever exists in our separate lives; we are restored to it whenever love lives in us. Love in all its forms in us is to be identified with Jesus Christ, and its life with His life. It is betrayed by the Judas in our own natures, and we suffer dereliction, willingly or unwillingly. The sacrifice of Calvary is everywhere and at all times, as is the supreme Rite by which we re-enact it.

But the utterances of Jesus are the literal commands of a state of love to which we generally have not come. Both our morality and our immorality make it difficult for us, when a burglar steals the silver spoons, to leave him at large and offer him the teapot too. In one place I think we have not taken the New Testament literally enough; when He exhorted us "Bear one another's burden" I believe He showed us a possibility which we have only dimly begun to understand. The knowledge that it is possible for us to take over the griefs and worries of others has, in the general world, still to be explored. It is, so discovered, a means towards the reference of all things to the Omnipotence. Our sins, though no doubt they should be frontally attacked, are rather to be left on one side in our strong preoccupation with other things, so that we never so much catch them up as outgo them, and in these things, as in all, intelligence is the moral duty of a Christian.

Creation is the mercy of God, and worthy to be loved. But love does not mean a love which finds any created thing necessary to its existence. It is a consuming fire, as in the great definitions of St. Thomas Aquinas: "Love regards good universally, whether possessed or not"; and "To love a person is nothing but to wish that person good." Yet although St. Thomas! and charge, Zion, may be the battle-cry of our hearts, that universal contemplation is the hardest achievement of our existence, and only the meeting of experience by both "This also is Thou" and its antithesis "Neither is this Thou," can help us to that lucidity. It is love existing semper, ubique, ab omnibus, as the Lady Julian of Norwich saw it. "Wouldst thou learn thy Lord's meaning in this thing? Learn it well, love was His meaning. What showed He thee? Love. Wherefore showed it He? For love. Who showed it thee? Love. What then can be amiss?" This, in its lucidity, I believe to be all the light of all our day.

25 September 1934

TWELVE

LIKE T. S. Eliot, Charles Williams is a Christian poet;
like Eliot, too, he is in communion with the Church
of England. Therein both seem to step apace to reconcile
the differences that for some hundred years have kept it a
stranger to Rome. For those who will admit the term,
"neo-Catholic" seems not out of place for both. But unlike Mr. Eliot, Williams has not struggled through any
mist clouding over a waste land of doubt. Here he makes
assurance certain:

> . . . The hypothesis which I first willed to accept, and
> which life confirms in me, is the Christian one, briefly:
> —the Deity of love and the Incarnation of Love, and I
> therefore formally accept the three Creeds, and the Chris-
> tian Faith (as declared in the rituals of the Church of
> England).

In his stream of song there is no "De Profundis"; neither
is there any "Dies Irae"; the mysteries of joy and those
of glory are a greater power to ecstasy. He sings of Advent
and of Christmas, of Easter and of Pentecost rather than
of the sufferings of the Passion. Does he intone a sorrow,
then he strikes a fundamental note revealing love exulting
and exalted. For Love is his "Summum Bonum." Should
one misunderstand his meaning, he speaks with clarity:

> . . . It is a consuming fire, but it is an intellectual fire,
> as in the great definitions of St. Thomas Aquinas: 'Love
> regards good universally, whether possessed or not'; and
> 'To love a person is nothing but to wish that person
> good.' . . . It is love existing *semper, ubique, ab omni-*
> *bus,* as the Lady Julian of Norwich saw it! 'Wouldst thou
> learn thy Lord's meaning in this thing? Learn it well,

love was His meaning. What showed He thee? Love. Who
showed it thee? Love. What then can be amiss?'

Believing love to be the light of all our day, as he
writes, he shows it is the life of all his own living. As a
lyrist, he cannot forego singing his credo. Yet he is not
content with singing it as a mere theory; he translates it
into the action of his song. And in his theory and practice
of Love, the poet is purely Christian. Holding the Incarnation as the *sine qua non* of our spiritual life here and
of our privilege of happiness in heaven, as the effect of
Infinite Love having assumed a nature by which it was
found in likeness a man, thus identifying Itself with
Christ, the God-Man, he implies later this further Catholic doctrine: Christ is present in us through sanctifying
grace as he is absent from us in its absence. This from
the poet in a letter to the writer:

> The Incarnation is the central event of our existence:
> an Act made inevitable by, and involved in, the First
> Creation. It is central to us in that it forever exists in
> our separate lives: we are restored to it whenever love
> lives in us. . . . It is betrayed by the Judas in our natures,
> and we suffer dereliction, willingly or unwillingly. The
> sacrifice of Calvary is everywhere and at all times, as is
> the Supreme Rite by which we re-enact it.

When Mr. Williams professes faith in the Three Creeds
and chants the mysteries and the revelation of Christian
orthodoxy, one wonders if he makes compromise when
he reverts to Pan, and when, in praise of Mary whom he
knows as "The maternal maid," he thinks upon the "Dian
of the Snows." "Old Saturn had her to his bride"; yet
"The Mother of Gods and Mother of Love is she." A
seepage of Paganism one feels as the poet on Easter morn
exalts the Victory of Love. While he would impress to

certainty that at the dawning of the sacred day the lions of Cybele were silent in their greetings, that the name of Adonis was mute on the lips of his wanton loves, that, on the other hand, all earth rings with the good tidings, that the Church runs to the Tomb, and that Spring proclaims a holiday, yet

> . . . she above
> Bowed down, his Mother and his Paramour,
> Unto that resurrection, while her train
> Of Syrian pontiffs sang their tale that hour:
> 'Hail, Attis born! hail, Attis born again!'[1]

But there is no compromise. Not that Charles Williams uses or misuses one for the sake of the other, but that he thinks Paganism is correlative with Christianity, that he understands it as expository. To him a pagan myth is as the parable that Christ used to explain a mystery. Both excite wonder in him. He is satisfied to probe no farther.

His "Ode for Easter Morning" might again mislead the intolerant. In it he exploits an opinion that he expresses with almost equal passion in "Orthodoxy." He would reach sanctity not only through Aquinasized love, but as Coventry Patmore did, through physical love Christianized. So firm is his faith that among contemporary poets he might be called the "Laureate of Nuptial Love." Like Patmore's, his theory is not the passion of Eros but of Eros Unknown. In practice as in principle he also guards and directs natural love to that degree of unification with Supreme Love whereby the soul becomes the "Sponsa Dei," the image of the Spouse of the Canticle, while of the physical being he says:

> O let me find my upper room in thee,
> Thou everlasting Easter! what a stone
> Of bare negation hast thou rolled away.[2]

Through human love he will climb his ladder of perfection. For him it is the consummation of all logic, of
all creeds and doctrines. It is the personification of orthodoxy, the refuter of heresies. It has the mark of the
Church: it is one, it is holy, it is Catholic, it is Apostolic.
And so addressing earthly love he says:

> In thee, in thee, revealed fair,
>   I end awhile my search,
> Thee, the One, Holy, Catholic,
>   And Apostolic Church.[3]

Though it is no substitute for devotion, for him it is a
road to the Way, the Truth, and the Life. Here he defines
it with love superlative:

> O new-conceived, doubly born,
> Immaculate in love,
> As She, that first of Christendoms,
> Deigns later dogmas prove,
> So by the kisses of thy mouth
> New laws and sanctities
> Teach! hark, thine honour, orthodox,
> Destroyer of heresies![4]

In closest union with Supreme Love he sings his intimacy with human love. The star that led to Greatest
Love leads him to a lesser love. In her presence, the singing
angel prompts him to "Ave," and love answering love, says
fittingly: "Ecce ancilla Domini!" Moving along the path
of holiest love, he goes on with allegory. Simeon's canticle
he hears once more amid the joys of nuptial love. Can
lesser love escape the sorrows incident to joy? Can the
Spouse be greater than the Master? For Williams here is
Simeon's prophecy fulfilled:

> . . . Dear.
> Livelong be our entreaty this,
> To feel the sword in every kiss![5]

Follow then manifestations of his love's soul, manifestations never known before. His public life, spent with her and for her, sees renewed in her the incident of Cana. The years find her transformed from clear, limpid water into the good wine kept for the end of the feast. And in state of deeper grace he sees her in vision or in dream, he knows not which, united with Love in the Host:

> In the True Body,
> Lo, your true face
> Looked to behold me.[6]

Again, his love would vision Christ in the beauty of her face. Actually the Lord of Love, he says, fulfills in her "His outer dwelling"; and his adoring love would make visible in her the Unseen Presence. And to show the pattern of their love as one of Heaven's choice, he introduces a Presence Immortal, the Spirit of Wedded Love, which maintains in eternity even outward union, Love's blessing on the oneness of their life on earth. For all similar loves, the Spirit promises this benediction:

> 'Hark, hark, all lovers triumph in the Christ,
> In him exult the wedded soul and blood,
> Who, kindling love, hath still for love sufficed.[7]

For an aureole of praise he gives her this tribute of fairest glory that will distinguish her in Heaven. Now art helps to create her loveliness, he tells her, but

> . . . when you go
> To keep the May of our New Year,
> Then all the world and heaven shall see
> Your pleasant gown of chastity.

. . . . .

> Only your finger still shall bear
> The single glowing ruby of
> Your passionate immortal love.[8]

Ever on an upward way by his "Scala Santa," Charles
Williams thinks not infrequently of the journey's end and
he speaks of it not tersely. "On Pilgrimage," bids all travelers to the Universal Good to walk apart from the mad-
ding crowd of unbelief, to fold their hands and make an
act of faith that is the credo of their heart. In it he would
suggest: "I believe in Love (ah me!), in love (ah, sweet!),
in Love." Spiritual Presences comfort him. They leave the
way along which he travels earth, a sacramental one only
to find that throughout the broad expanse of land,

> None to the heart shall contentment bind:
> One city alone to men is kind,
> That is seen and seen not, and kept of none,
> Yet allwhere hath ever to earth inclined.[9]

As the poet thinks of Sarras, as he calls the Perfect
City, his meditations pause upon the many mansions
there. Will the one he finds as he goes "House-hunting"
be modern or antique? Will he seek neighborhood con-
ditioned by his kind? Or will it be one like earth's affected
taste? Be what it will, the predilection will be to live in
the vicinity of God's Presence. There in sweet reverie,
he will muse upon the certainty with which he talked
on earth about those facts beyond the ken of mortal man.
But hampered by the material he questions happiness
away from "the towers, the gates of Westminster?" Yet,
withal, he has no mind of the forfeiture. Still some cares
there are:

> O let me pass, though I shall walk
> Least in your city, and your talk

> Shall never join, who only live
> To take your pardon, not to give.[10]

And what of his mannerisms, petty faults, and complaints which will persist, he fears, to show themselves ironically his own? However, they will not be to his undoing, but serve always, he feels, a "parrot for me with its hideous squawk." Likewise, thwarted hopes in him will not be grievous witness against his soul. Passing over bridges impassable in life, he sees from an eminence, "o'er a gentle tide, . . . futile works,—lo there on the other side." In peace and solitude then he has his satisfaction.

Moving always in love, the poet turns from the argument of souls unified temporally through marriage, a fitting symbol of the spiritual relation of Christ and the soul, to a defence of that bond which holds the Republic to Deity. Similarly, as in wedded union, their consequent interrelation is as a seal signing and appraising deep worth. In the nuptial of Faith and the Republic, he rises to ecstasy in feeling that Heaven reveals itself Republican in professing this trinity of mind: "One, indivisible, and free." There in that Utopian Republic, joy abounds when freed from "prince and shah," the people are brothers all vowed to the riding. And then to roam the ideal comes this his dearest hope: that England may ere long resound the strain, those

> Notes of the only True!
> O Christian creed of deity
>
> .   .   .   .   .
>
> One, indivisible, and free,
> The triple formula![11]

Sarras is, obviously, his Republic eternized, the Perfect City. There kin are truly kindred. When the beginning of eternal ecstasy takes place, those marked with the triple insignia will lead on in long procession to the Prince of Brotherhood, born of a woman and still Divine.

It is nothing wonderful that the poet lays bare the heritage of his Ideal. Hence, Apostasy and the Republic confront each other in verbal play. Identifying itself with Love, the Republic is the Fair, the Perfect City, in nature human and divine. Unseen in reality, it conceives and brings forth the thoughts of men in government; it cherishes a constant hope amid the hopelessness of men; it is a part of all construction; it visions all things in their entirety; it rebuilds the destruction of enemies. It has suffered death, annihilation, to be a surety for men. To all men, it is native, free, and equal. It affects not their choice, but, if men elect its way, the Republic stands, a God; if they refuse, as a dream it passes on. Their acceptance makes the heavens reject them not; their non-acceptance makes clay their rest. And all this is its mission, for it is

> I, Love, who only can a man befriend
> If he be glad thereto.[12]

Apostasy is ready always with retort. It is Love's counterforce, a foe to unity, to freedom, and to equality. All good has it destroyed; all virtue has it tempted in pretext of a nearer good. And now it renews the Tempted Christ in its plea to feed the poor. Unjustly it calls on Justice and challenges Love to manifest itself for love. Men it portrays as constant only to apostasy. And it is in that mind that the Fair Republic has reality. Thus time goes on and with it man to certain death and Love with him. To which Love makes willing answer:

> When this opaque world shall by me be lit,
>   And I be manifest,—not to destroy,
> Not to destroy, but to transfigure it
>   With uncreated joy.

Then visibly shall I be bound in walls,
    Sink in foundations and in towers grow high,
Then shall I stand and shine while no stone falls,
    There shall be naught but I.[13]

There are other poems holding Mr. Williams' faith in Love as the soul of our life. To him in spiritual crises Love has given hope and safety through the whisperings of a voice scattering darkness. Meekness and humility of heart he knows to be compatible with love. Is he the proud man turned from Love's feast? Self-examination prompts:

O then be wise, sweet!
    Now, let's go bare,
At the poor's feast, Love's feast,
    To have place there.[14]

And for a consummation of desire, the craving that drives unsatisfied love to that Highest which alone is satisfying, he utters the inevitable cry, ". . . let us look on God and die, Feel him, one shock, and end! We would see Love!" All that Love has center and circumference in a Little Child, Who was in Perfection both God and Man. In harmony with the Athanasian creed, Charles Williams sings:

O who can doubt the Perfect Whole
    In his eternal trysting,—
Love, of the reasonable soul
    And human flesh subsisting.[15]

Desiring good to all men, his own theory of love, he exhorts all to this belief: salvation and sanctification follow only in the pure, universal, and humble pursuit of that Little Child. Expect the pitfalls and snares on the way, he says; give credence, if needs be, to other intuitions, but always feel this piercing truth: "O beata Trinitas! O et Verbum Caro!"

This redeeming love of the Godhead finds repetition in each of Mr. Williams' volumes. Christmas, the feast of Love, finds his heart, his mind, and his soul journeying to Bethlehem, where Mary having vision of her lost Child restored, sings in canticle of joy to his strayed soul. Sarras might have rejoiced that day as when on Easter morn, it cries in heavenly bliss:

> Tidings, behold a
> Townsman is born.[16]

Christ's Mother he praises in the words of "Ecclesiasticus." The prophets sang her as Mother of fair love, Knowledge and fear and holy hope!" Then, as now, they were not merely lyric: Mary, Mother of the Word substantiated Beauty. The Immaculate One, he implores to keep him in her entreaties with Divine Love. Neither must she cease from continuous intercession that all life and all song be Marian in magnificence. He knows that in the town of Sarras she goes on in love with Peter, John, and Michael, as the Maid and Mother

> As when she rinsed the cup and can
> For blessed Joseph, a labouring man,
> And God, a Carpenter.[17]

The passion, Christ's signal love-deed for mankind, Mr. Williams knows is renewed daily through sin, yet a resurrection is, likewise, in sequence and through it Love grants peace. But, among those who meet Love as He moves to bless with peace, there are those who, like the Apostles, are still incredulous even in face of the Risen One and in His hearing. The Mysteries of Pentecost, another Love feast, when the Church received her sublime mission, and of the Ascension when

> To his profoundest origin
> Love manifested yearns,[18]

fill him with song. So do Magdalene, Stephen, the Confessors, the Martyrs, and the holy souls. He prays them all. He would go further, too, than ritual. Canonically as well as popularly, the poet would give just observance to Valentine, Benedict, Cecilia, Catherine, Agnes, Augustine, the masters of theology, those saints in

> Love's divine science and the fount of song:
> To whom the Angelic Doctor does belong.[19]

Within the articles of his belief is the Real Presence. Now as in those days of early Christian faith when hearts sought comfort in the Institution of Highest Love, the fulfillment of the Master's revelation: "This is my body, this is my blood." "The Theological Virtues" claim the tribute of his heart. Greater than either Faith or Hope is that which has

> . . . no name,
> Title or rites, but only his who draws
> All souls in thee, O motion of his laws. . . .

This Charity or Love is Justice too. He knows it weighs all things in the balances of Heaven, but Love, the saving love of Christ, he hopes, will outweigh even any doom.

ANNA HEMPSTEAD BRANCH:

Lover of man and of the mystic

LETTER FROM ANNA HEMPSTEAD BRANCH

I wrote In the Beginning Was the Word *a good many years ago when we were spending the summer at our old House in New London.*

Higher criticism in the mouth of a distinguished preacher and Biblical scholar had recently stated that the Bible although written by various men and groups of men at various times and places, although not a book with unity of purpose, not written under very special or Divine guidance, was still "good for warning, exhortation, and instruction."

I found that I "missed the Bible" in the sense that I had always accepted it, as a book of peculiar and unique inspiration, good for more than "warning, exhortation, and instruction." I felt a little suspicious of all this higher criticism with its constant alarums of "internal evidence." I thought there might be other kinds of internal evidence finer and subtler in their character—perceptible not so much to the intellect as to the interior perception—rhythms and cadences of movement and emotion, a pattern of thought and episode—the sort of internal evidence that might appeal to a penetrative imagination rather than to the scrutiny of mere scholarship.

About this time Percy Mackaye's masque of Celibacy *was presented in New York City by different social groups and then proceeded on its two years' journey across country, acted in many places by various groups. "Here," I thought—"is the master mind of a poet, acting through his pageant upon different individuals in different times and places; it sweeps whole towns into its significance. It is grown out of the intellects and wills and emotions of multitudes yet always reveals behind it a master mind, a master personality which is, as far as these presentations are concerned, out of space and out of time."*

I also reflected upon the masque of New London devised by one of the instructors in the English Department at Connecticut College. The plan of it—the general outline—was her own, but under her guidance each of her four classes in English was to act in detail one act—to be made a part, during four successive years, of the Commencement Exercises, in various parts of the campus such as were appropriate in setting. Then at the end of the four years all the classes were to convene at a reunion and the whole masque was to be enacted.

Here indeed was a comparison. I cogitated upon the statement of that clergyman who had decided that the Bible was still good for "warning, exhortation, and instruction," but who had also decided that since it was undoubtedly written by many men in various times and places it therefore could not have any essential unity, nor could it have been written under one inspiration.

But here was Percy Mackaye's masque and here was the masque of New London, and even since these were actuated and operated by minds which were, as far as these events were concerned, super-intelligences, might it not be possible after all that the far greater mind of a more interior master had indeed devised and inspired the Great Book imparting to it essential unity of his own invisible and profoundly spiritual organism?

After all, who could tell whether the Bible had any essential unity or whether it did not have, until he had read it through as concentratedly and as rapidly as possible, instead of catching at a few random text or even with a devoted and scholarly consideration of its chapters and its books.

I therefore decided, somewhat blindly, to read the Bible through as rapidly as possible to see what happened.

It was hot summer weather. During the period in which I dedicated myself to reading the Bible through at the most rapid possible rate, I used to rise each morning at about three o'clock and in the early morning silence would run downstairs, barefooted into the dew, breathe the fresh air of dawn, look at the stars, then upstairs to my own room again. There I would light three candles. It was too warm to enjoy a big old-fashioned oil lamp. In the old homestead at this time there was no electricity. Then I would read until breakfast time, and after breakfast, till the middle of the morning, when forsaking the Book, I would walk three miles down to the beach, go for a swim, and walk three miles back again, reaching home in time for our noon dinner. After dinner I would read until supper time, and after supper time late into the evening until very often I did, as the poem says, fall asleep with my head on the page. Sometimes people say to me—did you include the genealogies? Yes, I did.

My eyes gave out in the middle of this crusade so I had to rest them for a couple of days. I might with perfect veracity say I read the Bible through in eight days. After the interruption I resumed with the big family Bible which had a larger print than my own Bible had. I shall always remember this reading of the Bible as one of the most exciting events of my life. The poem is by no means exaggerated in its expression. It is, of course, one of interior perception not of outward experience. I might have said more than I did. Perhaps sometime I will relate the episode more in detail. Suffice it to say that I consider this Book a biological process and the reading of it in any profound interpretation of the word as a moment in evolution.

March 26, 1933

THIRTEEN

ALOOF from the worldly, yet devoted to settlement work at Christodora House in the heart of New York City, Anna Hempstead Branch fulfilled her high vocation as a Christian poet. Her consecration to Beauty was early. A voice heard in a dream moved her with this depth of thought: "For in those days the poets were not forgetful of their high calling." That prompting, and the heritage of a New England vision of Beauty that transcends the earth, a vision that sees Beauty in symbol, that longs to share it with one's fellowmen, and one which, in its perfection, leads self to lose itself in Love, combine in Miss Branch to make her a "Lover of Man and of the Mystic."

Held by song inspired by the Creator of Rhythm, Anna Hempstead Branch felt bound to serve her gift. As a young poet, at times when she would have elected silence, the commanding presence of song disturbed her soul. When she held a pause, "Divinity" spoke through it:

> For when my thoughts are silent every one
> . . . Thy speech falls on me subtle as the sun.[1]

Sleep she invited to give rest to winged thought, but there was to be no repose from singing, for another voice broke forth:

> . . . His hand has wrought
> A sound in thy soul's raiment thou dost hear,
> Poor child, that cannot rid thyself of singing.[2]

Song-haunted, did she not even at any early age feel that her way in the world was to be of the elect? One finds her ready answer when she sings:

In other orbits do my paths belong
And other hands will beckon me before
God sets a wonder upon all my days. . . .[3]

Thus has she always moved among men with a singleness of purpose: spending herself in the truly Christian sense to lift man's spirit from the dross of the natural, while she herself transcends earth, searches the land of the mystic, and there conceives her song, as one of her titles suggests: "It Sprang from an Abyss of Light."

That mystic light shed hallowed radiance on her in early life. Like another cloud of glory, it trailed her existence. She says:

. . . a might
Pursues my soul in flashes of long light
. . . Till my whole spirit melts into refrain.[4]

Has not its brilliance suffused her soul and made her a truant from all that is not the symbolic or the mystic in Beauty?

Thus the poetry of Anna Hempstead Branch seems lighted from afar. The poet has looked into her heart and has written what she found there: love of the mystic. But in pledging love to the intuitive, the ideal, she has not forsworn love of the practical and the real, for she is also a lover of man, but not in the humanitarian sense merely. Where plain philanthropy ends, Love begins. Miss Branch's devotion for mankind lies deeper than the external needs of social welfare. It is, therefore, the attar of love. It follows then, that, in her high faith, even amid the drab and the gray days in life, she can see good in everything. And a voice of a higher strain makes assurance doubly sure: "Look out, look out! Angels are drawing nigh!" Then comes her act of love:

Then my slow burdens leave me, one by one,
And swiftly does my heart arise and run
Even like a child, while loveliness goes by—
And common folk seem children of the sky,
And common things seem shaped of the sun.[5]

The faces of these common folk, wan with poverty,
grief, and toil, are a balm for her hurt soul. The cold
harmony of a daisy field cannot evoke that spirit of Christian love that calms a heart astir. Faith alone, a mere ritual
of words, is again no help to her undoing. Love must
be a practise as well as a belief. So Anna Hempstead Branch
must, as she says, "plunge in the fountain of its living
blood." From her theory of love, the shame that she assumes for the sins of Manhattan comes now in proper
sequence. Remote from merely the humanitarian view,
the attitude that would stress the woe of the bleeding feet
of the wandering woman rather than the child she nursed
upon her "ruined breast," the poet suffers the pain of
remorse in having let sin become red as scarlet when the
public conscience pretends to be white as snow. In further
witness of her love for man's soul, she begs to atone for
the sins of Manhattan, the Scarlet Woman:

. . . Is there no voice to move—
No hand to smite us? Even for this I pray—
Some terrible scourging that we have let the day
Darken around us while we saw thee rove.[6]

There is no tone of blame, for, purely Christian, she
loves the sinner, not his sin. This favorite idea finds anal-
ogy, too, in the unguarded sweetness and innocent vulgar-
ity of the shop girl parading waste and want, defying the
conventional, and challenging early ruin. Pity finds no rebuke for the daring though guileless child and bids those

who have starved for their soul's glory throw the first
stone for

> Poet and prophet in God's eyes
> Make no more perfect sacrifice.
>
> Who knows before what inner shrine
> She eats with them the bread and wine?
>
> .   .   .   .
>
> So let us love and understand—
> Whose hearts are hidden in God's hand.[7]

Miss Branch repeats this motif somewhat when she confesses that perfect love comes only through a sympathy, a
complete understanding through a sharing of grief.
Whereas she once thought "that healing came from the
angels' wings," experience has taught that the greatest
joy is in suffering nobly borne: hands bruised and feet
tired with honest toil.

As a lover of man, the use of money is sacred to Anna
Hempstead Branch; its abuse, sacrilegious. Gained
through guilt, trading childhood, dulling conscience, and
dimming vision, money renews the crime of Cain. Vehe-
mently, the old cry, "Am I my brother's keeper?" will strike
the heart of God when the traffickers in gold present their
true accounts of flesh and blood.

Remembering injustice to the wage-slave, Miss Branch
would stamp out from the coin the eagle, emblem of freedom, and would carve thereon the tragedies of labor or

> Some solemn accusation that shall declare,
> "Ye serve the rich, the poor ye do not spare,
> The Unpaid Toiler has not been set free."[8]

or such a screed as would connote the shining gold as
the urn holding the ashes of one whose dreams were yet
undreamed, whose deeds were yet undone.

Even in the commodities bought with this rare coin, the poet sees the cruelty of greed. In the weaving of the fabric, in its intricate design, and in the obscurity of color she sees "Medea's wreath" and the oppression of the tyrant. Yet, while men buy and sell; while, in the constant change and interchange of values, heaven and earth would seem one market of trade through the barter of rich and unknown "bales of merchandise . . . stretched upon the counters of the air" with the golden discs that make the splendor of the sky; and while the spirits of the ether would seem to be the masters of exchange, still "The Laboring Man strives up the starry Hill."

Apart from the abuse which money through greed excites, Anna Hempstead Branch finds high symbolism in the medium of exchange. The circle of the coin is a type to her of that greater circle of the earth guided by the Power that governs birth and increase in the natural order. And on these rings that propagate and develop in the world of finance, she feels the "presence of the Power with Wings." Their golden covering brings her to the robe that folds

> . . . round the God
> Whose flesh is music and whose glittering rod
> Ruleth the earth with his strict numberings.[9]

The coin itself assumes a precious dignity as a symbol of that brighter Coin that so shone once in the open sky and led three shepherds to a greater Treasure in the heart of earth. There the Coin in mystic light shone for the Three Wise Men "And in a woman's bosom nestled bright,"

> So in a manger dark as any purse
> They found the God who is the Universe.[10]

That God served as a medium of exchange when He paid the price of man's sin. Coin, then, truly used, is, to Anna Hempstead Branch, sacramental, the living Christ. It holds the shape, the sign, forever, of the Word: "This money is a sacramental thing." Further, "Beware the Presence of the Bread and Wine."

Awed by this sense, the high sanctity of exchange in the Person of Divinity as barter, Miss Branch passes from the world of symbols, pale and weak, to intimate union with that candor, that beauty, and that triumph that shines from the brow "Of the Great Lover whereto I am bride." In His Presence she feels not the comfort of evening dew, but the thrust of the sword-blade to open to her sight "fresh splendor . . . and a virgin birth." Moved by this grace, she seeks repeatedly in flight of self the loci of Divinity. There must she be or else meet utter death.

For the all-embracing love of Christ, she finds a happy symbol. Stressing Love's power to pierce all things, she sees it as a kiss facing a gale on a bitter cold night. The sign is small, flame-wreathed

> Like an archangelic child,
> No bigger than a blossom,
> That an angel great and mild
> Might nourish in her bosom.[11]

This mystic symbol cleaves the sun, the moon, frost, and a prison wall. It clings to the lips of the prisoner; it flies to the breast of a woman where it rests as a child; it blinds one and maddens another; it moves some to pity; and it escapes others. Above a church-spire it shines a lovely blue; over the sea, white, but over a courthouse, red. It warms the sky and folds the earth in its breast. Then

All things shone
And all things were at rest.

The Angels saw it shine
With its countenance of flame.
They threw off their crowns
For "Holy" was its Name.[12]

In the presence of this Love, "the Marriage Supper Of the Son and the Bride," the poet visions the meaning of purely Christian Love which seeks to include all creation and to transform it by union with Christ's Mystical Body.

Dust is a symbol to the poet of all that earth can give. Into the hands of a court fool she places, as he says, "the sum and substance of this world": the dust of which it is made and to which it will return. Again, the three who slept and dreamed of a pet fault while the Master prayed in the garden, prefigure attachment to sin even among the elect. Nor does she let the Beloved John flee the tempter. This from "The Sleep in Gethsemane":

"Nay," quoth John, "but I'll take no rest!"
He thought that he lay on the Lord Christ's breast,
But it turned to a maid's that he loved the best!
    O Lord, pity us!

Again, order is symbolic to the poet of the Cleanness of God. Thus the plain task of shining brazen pots and iron pans and of washing earthen floors assumes a noble dignity. In their forms of brass, iron, brick, or stone, she sees a primal splendor fresh from the Hands of the Great Shaper. As she polishes the pans, she offers this prayer:

Whoever makes a thing more bright,
He is an angel of all light.
Therefore let me spread abroad
The beautiful cleanness of my God.[13]

The symbolic leads one to the mystical in beauty. In her desire to share the beauty that lies beyond the natural, Anna Hempstead Branch would leave the limits of her own self. Renouncing thought and will, and having vision only, she beholds a brilliant likeness;

> That from its Heaven searches into mine
> And bends to me, even as a star to star.[14]

In the same mood she mounts the watch tower of her soul. There in the silence broken only by the Voice of God dropping like "dew upon the ground," she knows that she is set apart for Beauty. The sense grows stronger when, at night, Heaven seems to stoop to her. Is it a feigned love for earth that raises this plaint:

> O Paradise, depart!
>> Why bidest thou with me?
> Thy petals sting my face that drop
>> From off thy Holy Tree.[15]

For in later years, with the spirit of a New England mystic, she sings of the Voice that spoke to her soul throughout "Three Days! Three Nights." Joyously and solemnly she heard it sing with "mystic tenderness." With mirth, peace, and love it filled her soul, as wondrously she listened to its "passionate utterance! Speech divine!" Then she knew that Love Itself had embraced her heart. She knew, too, that by that very act Love had sealed her consecration "unto the Lord."

She is the Transcendentalist again in "Seamless Garment." God and the Zodiac, His creation, she does not sever. Man must rise to the dignity of starry glory, must love wholeness that he may not tear

> The seamless garment, nor rend the crystal bars.
> Oh, cry not out upon the Shining Fish—

Say not, "This is the Scorpion, this the Bear"—
But say "here is the god among the stars."

A crystal, too, brings her the light of God. Through the prismatic colors she sees "A spiritual, a more interior thing. It is the love of Shapes," of patterns that come and go as they shine through the crystal lamp of beauty and through each other and then merge perfectly. This vision leads to great imaginings: the stars with highest ecstasy, the passion of Deity, and nicety of power "embrace . . . The hieroglyph, the alphabetic sign." To the Transcendentalist that is the Alpha and Omega, God. Rightly may earth claim the Love of Divinity:

> Now let the cosmic love of gods be claimed.
> Here is the sacred festival whereby
> A marriage weds a marriage in the sky
> With ceremonials no priest has named.
> The Lord's own body brighter than the sun
> Makes one the two who each is three in one.[16]

But in the last two verses Miss Branch thinks purely Christian thought, as she sings the Trinity.

A poet, naturally Christian, Anna Hempstead Branch strengthens her work with the human sweetness and cosmic light of her belief. Tribute to Mary she gives in the praise of Watteau, court painter, who, defying royalty, presents to a danseuse slippers on which he has painted his masterpiece: a Madonna, the Virgin. "Dance," he says

> Upon those little satin shoes are painted
> What made night perfect and on a barren day
> Shed light.
>
> Dance! Dance! I bid you dance!
> Forever and forever! O Virgin Mary!—
> Dance! Dance![17]

Mary is always the Mother of Christ as God. This truth of dogma she professes even as she lyricizes a black kitten: a symbol to her of fun in Heaven, for

> . . . only God's Mother getting to sleep
> The Eternal Babe would think to make
> A little foolish thing like you![18]

Furthermore, on Judgment Day, Mary will tell "The funny things that Jesus does." When she recalls the thoughts of a little brother in religion, as he lies down at night, invoking the four evangelists who guard his bed, it is the little Christ of whom he wants to dream.

> Saying "Christ, Christ, Christ!" to bring him near.
> If he were little, would he hear?
> And would his mother tell him nay
> If I should ask him out to play?[19]

In this spirit of love for the Christ-Child, the poet observes the ceremony of the Christmas Candle: Christ, the Light of the World, coming to illumine earth's darkness and to dwell as Love in hearts that love. Note the poet's love of the mystic here:

> Now—in the Seventh Year—the Flame
> Transmutes the letters of the Name—
> Which, shining like the Snow White Dove
> Brings festivals of Fire and Love.[20]

To Death and the soul after death she gives place in her singing. Paradise is all happiness. Its symbol on earth is a mother's face. "Those only laugh—those folk that die." And happier yet is this interpretation:

> Heaven is exquisite with fun—
> The laughter of the Three-in-One.[21]

From Purgatory a soul returns with the message that alms

given to the poor in behalf of the suffering ones release
them from their prison. Penance, likewise, lessens their
pain. Sorrow, suffering in silence, a cross carried for Love
takes captive souls to Heaven. Furthermore, the cross,
symbol of supreme love, would sacrifice Heaven itself.
Speaking for Lazarus, she says:

> A great desire led me out alone
> From those assured abodes of perfect bliss.
> One thing more fair than they, more keen, more sweet! . . .

> *The Crowd*
> What was it, Lazarus? Let us share that thing!
> What was it, brother, thou didst see?

> *Lazarus*
> A cross.[22]

In faëry, even, Miss Branch's faith prevails over fancy.
No beauty is comparable to Mary's. Characters invoke the
Virgin against the elementals. Again, fairies depart under
the sign of the cross, or it transforms them despite their
willingness. A fairy says:

> But a chance has come upon me!
> And God, that bids nothingness to serve,
> Has bound me, that was nothing. . . .
> . . . So even upon me,
> The denial of his Being, emptiness,
> The Shaper has laid hold, so I must be
> A word out of his mouth to say "He is"![23]

Here also the poet tells the power of prayer:

> There are hands
> Strong and invisible as thine own spells,
> And they move all things, even the heart of God.
> The Hands of prayer.[24]

Symbolic of her Christian faith is her belief in God as the Revealer of the Bible. Urged by adverse criticism of the Book as the Inspired Word, Miss Branch undertook to read the Bible through in the hope that by so reading a poet might perceive One Unity, One spirit, where historical critics saw only what they were trained to see. Rigorously reading and resting six hours at a stretch, she read the Bible through and emerged with this triumphant Faith:

> I consider this book a biological process and the reading of it—in my profound interpretation of that word—as a grand moment in evolution.

In the poem celebrating this experience, she says:

> For a great wind blows
> Through Ezekiel and John.
> They are all one flesh
> That the Spirit blows upon.[25]

Love of Christ, the Highest Beauty, lifts Miss Branch to almost mystical experience. Wholly possessed by the desire of the personal embrace of Christ, she feels transformed even by the desire for union. In her thought of Love's Beauty inebriating her soul there comes a beauty known only in Love's Presence. She sings to Divinity:

> . . . when the sweetness of your love
> Beholds a grace in me,
> It is as if a golden dove
> Lit in a wild-wood tree.[26]

But her triumph in mysticism comes when she plays her "Strange and Lovely Game." Caught by the splendor of shining whiteness, she loses self in Love that holds her a complete captive. As "a shining shape, A daughter of the sun," she runs to the Heart of her Lord. She tells Him all her hopes, her fears for

The lover of all playing things
Is ever quick to hear.

  . . . . .

He showed me how to weave a crown
Of exquisite desire,
Blossomed and leaved with living flame
And garlandings of fire.[27]

In token of her consecration to Beauty, of her love of the
symbolic and the mystic, she seals her innocent play with

He plucked me apples of the sun
From off a golden bough,
Then left a wreath of laughing light
Around my happy brow.[28]

THOMAS S. JONES, JR.:

The singer of the perfect city

Extracts from

LETTER FROM THOMAS S. JONES, JR.

*For weeks I have wanted to tell you of early influences:
All my grandparents were British. Mother's father, born
in Norwich, came from the Blackett family of Newcastle—
a family closely associated with Durham, and thus to Lindis-
farne. Her mother was born at Castle Martyr on the
Shannon, not far from Clonmacnoise. Father's mother was
born on Holyhead, the most sacred island of the Druids—
so the influence of the past is clear here. Father's father
was born in Wales, not far from Chester. You can see from
this how my background was that of the Church of Glastonbury, Sarum, and Columba: Clonmacnoise and Durham
being the poles of the latter.*

*I was born in a little country town in New York State,
on the edge of the Adirondacks, but opposite to my grandmother's was a little English Church, exquisite in design,
with its high cabled roof, topped by a lovely Celtic Cross!!,
and with a charming tower of three stages, crowned with
three graceful finials. Exquisite taste! I would lie in bed at
my grandmother's, and, through the open door, look out
on this little church in its green leaf-setting, shot with
sunlight. It was always a symbol of beauty, peace, and
love. Mother loved it—every bit of it: its altar most of all.
(And now the memorial Cross upon the altar is to her
memory.) Here she made her first Communion, as I did
mine. Only the most beautiful memories are about it: this
was the beginning.*

411 West 115 Street
New York City
February 26, 1931

Dear Sister Mary James,

I am enclosing the second copy of a sonnet on John Donne, written yesterday: Dr. Henry Wells of the graduate school at Columbia has the first copy, and at this very hour he is reading this poem, with the others on Herbert, Vaughan, and Crashaw, to his class.

Gladly shall I inscribe any book you send me. The Lamb is only waiting paper, now in customs, on which to print the book. You may obtain copies, certainly a week or so, but I shall send you the first copies. (Of course, you noted the reversal of the want e in Niquolet: this has been corrected.)

For years I have wanted to tell you of early influences: All my grandparents were British. Mother's father, born in Norwich came from the 'Black Irish,' a very possible--a family closely associated with Durham and thus inexhaustible. True, Her mother was born at Castle Martyr on the Shannon, not far from Clonmacnoise. Father's mother was born on Holyhead, the most sacred island of the Druids-- so the influence of the past is clear here. Father's father was from Wales, not far from Chester. You can see from this how my background was that of the Church of Glastonbury, Sarum, and Columba: Clonmacnoise and Durham being the poles of the latter.

I was born in a little country town in New York state, on the edge of the Adirondacks. In my grandmother's was a little English Church, exquisite. It had a fully Gothic design, with an old high cabled roof, topped by a lovely Celtic Cross; and with a charming tower of three stages, crowned with three graceful finials. Exquisite taste! I would lie in bed at my grandmother's, and, through the open door, look out on this little church in its green leaf-setting, shot with sunlight. It was always a symbol of beauty, peace, and love. Mother loved it --very bit of it: its altar most of all. (And now the memorial brass upon the altar is to her memory.) Here she made her first Communion, as I did mine. Only the most beautiful memories are about it: this was the beginning.

Another early memory that made a great impression on me was the first time I experienced the service of Benediction. I was very young, and our loved maid took me to her Church. I could not have been much more than ten, but the whole scene of infinite beauty and loveliness is as fresh this moment, as it

was thirty-five years ago. And the very moment of Benediction is the most vivid of all: I remember the lowered lights, the hush, the lifted Host in the golden monstrance, as if it were last night.

The next great influence was my mother's death, falling on the morning of Holy Thursday: she was buried Easter. Even in the little country town where I was born. Thus the day of the Last Supper was burned into my spirit; and I suppose this incident combined with the natural love of the Arthurian legends, deep in my blood. Here was my connection with James Lane Allen. Shortly after mother's death, I read The Choir Invisible and although I did not know it then, here was the crying out of the old stories, the Morte Darthur, which I was later to know so well.

Then came school and college: Thornton Jenkins, of Malden, who used to read me Wordsworth and Browning --a splendid man, and one of the finest influences of my youth: the next year, Hiram Corson, good friend of the Brownings and Tennyson, with who I took courses throughout my four years.-- He certainly was the greatest influence at this time. But at this very time I was with Edward Bradford Titchnor, who was under Pater at Oxford, and Charles Mellen Tyler, a very saint, with whom I took my courses in Eastern religions. He was a dear friend of Max Müller. Also, at this time I saw much of a friend, who was a great lover of William Morris and was expert in making manuscripts on vellum, with color and gold-leaf.

Next came the deep interest in contemporary poetry, during this period Jessie Rittenhouse, Lizette Reese, Edith Thomas, Thomas Tolmar, Henry Mills Allen, and James Lane Allen, came to be dear friends.

I heard much of Louise Guiney at this time, and through Fiona Macleod, the knowledge of Iona came to me. Then came Columba, the actual Glastonbury-- and my travels. The rest you can easily trace and put together.

I shall gladly expand anything you might wish, but the key-points are all proposed above.

Gratefully yours,

[signature]

Another early memory that made a great impression on me was the first time I experienced the service of Benediction. I was very young, and our loved maid took me to her Church. I could not have been much more than ten, but the whole scene of infinite beauty and loveliness is as fresh this moment, as it was thirty-five years ago. And the very moment of Benediction is the most vivid of all: I remember the lowered lights, the hush, the lifted Host in the golden monstrance, as if it were last night.

The next great influence was my mother's death, falling on the morning of Holy Thursday: She was buried Easter Even in the little country town where I was born. Thus the day of the Last Supper was burned into my spirit; and I suppose this incident combined with the natural love of the Arthur legends, deep in my blood. Here was my connection with James Lane Allen. Shortly after mother's death, I read The Choir Invisible, *and although I did not know it then, here was the crying out of the old stories, the* Morte D'Arthur, *which I was later to know so well.*

Then came school and college: Thornton Jenkins, of Malden, who used to read me Wordsworth and Browning —a splendid man, and one of the finest influences on my youth; the next year, Hiram Corson, good friend of the Brownings and Tennyson, with whom I took courses throughout my four years. He certainly was the greatest influence at this time. But at this very time I was with Edward Bradford Titchnor, who was under Pater at Oxford, and Charles Mellen Tyler, a very saint, with whom I took my courses in Eastern religions. He was a dear friend of Max Muller. Also, at this time I saw much of a friend, who was a great lover of William Morris and was expert in making manuscripts on vellum, with color and gold-leaf.

Next came the deep interest in contemporary poetry. During this period Jessie Rittenhouse, Lizette Reese, Edith

Thomas, Thomas Mosher, Henry Mills Alden, and James Lane Allen, came to be dear friends.

I heard much of Louise Guiney at this time, and through Fiona MacLeod, the knowledge of Iona came to me. Then came Columba, the actual Glastonbury—and my travels. The rest you can easily trace and put together.

February 26, 1931

FOURTEEN

THOMAS S. JONES, JR., burned with a passion for perfection. A poet of a loving heart, seeking only the fairest and worshipping, therefore, the something afar, he dedicated that heart without reserve to the Ideal. His work is, then, another Canticle of Love. In all the liturgy of his song, one hears a haunting call, "an ancestral call, a nostalgia for the homeland of his people." But the call soars beyond earth, beyond the verge of time and space. It is a homesickness for heaven that harmonized his thought so perfectly with angels, saints, and joys known only to the Lovers of the Light. It set him apart as "Singer of the Perfect City": the spiritual city in which perfect thoughts and ideals sing in all the color and glory of the desire for the hearts of great lovers and dreamers who burned to find Perfection: the prophets and philosophers, the sainted scholars and early scientists, the martyrs and the missionaries, the followers and crusaders of the Light: symbols of the Perfect Lover.

That Love did set him apart to seek the fairest, the poet felt when he sang in 1911 this solemn pledge:

> Only to burn at Thy unknown desire—
> For this alone has Song been granted me.
> Upon Thy altar burn me at Thy will;
> All wonders fill
> My cup, and it is Thine;
> Life's precious wine
> For this alone: for Thee.[1]

His consecration to his Ideal was life-long. As he entered upon his dedicated work, he heard a Voice from the silences. And he answered it through life with praise of "Him Who is the Perfect Friend."

The life of adoration which he chose to serve he saw clearly around him. He saw it first in nature: in the rose, Dante's "perfect flower." Significantly, he called his first volume: *The Rose-Jar*. It held his fascination for the Ideal that lasts beyond "the smart of time and death." That Ideal his mother's love helped gloriously to inspire and to cherish. He saw perfection as well in nature's other beauties. The calm of low-toned winds sheltered within a cloistered place, silence held in the hollow of the hills, truth kept white in the firm abode of trees, faith maintained amid the homely peace of ember-glow, dreams redreamed through the stillness of dusk, deeds undone in the flotsam and jetsam of ebb-tide, man's dissolution in the wind-blown petals of the rose, and the nearness of God in the vastness of the sea—all are symbols of the life of adoration. In 1911, he says:

> It is not far, the life of adoration,
> . . . Each dawn has known the mystic elevation,
> And twilight burns pale tapers in the sky.[2]

A pine grove becomes a cathedral with high embowed roof of green and aisles wind-swept for organ music. Incense from the leafy fragrance lends sanctity to the air; the sunset adds the glow of storied windows, and then

> The dusk creeps on . . . softly a twilight bell . . .
> And now, the altar-candle of a star.[3]

In a quiet vale hallowed with the solemn song of birds and branches, he finds Him Whom his soul loveth,

> . . . a brooding Presence that makes each moment
> A benediction;[4]

while mountains, touched only by the eagle's wing, keep virgin splendor and hold in sacred trust the radiance of the Pierced Hands and Feet.

His mother's death, loss of health, and exile to the hills press immortality upon his heart, and lead his soul on in the quest for the something afar. The rhythm felt in nature through birth, life, and death in the flora, measured to the roll of the seasons; the rhythm of sun-rise and sunset sealing day after day, of winds and tides lapping the shores of space, of morning and evening dew freshening the flowers—all these veiled his eyes in awe at

> Hint of some great mystery
> Past the outposts of the stars![5]

Again, the sway of lilacs in the rain and a haze filming nature's loveliness speak heaven to his loving heart. An isle remote, an isle of Avalon, is the threshold of unearthly joy; lonely moorlands give promise of a greater peace; the wearied stretch of roads moves to an end that "is not in vain"; and all things of earth that stand the test of time are proofs of "what may be." "Joyous Gard" has helped him to a vision of the future. Through it he has looked upon the Grail, and, here, in life, has he felt the ecstasy of the Perfect City. Spring, too, with its renewing power of beauty and its remembrance of old friends with whom he shared its rapture, bodes the glory of "that perpetual spring," and days that have brought fulfilment of desire through prayer are gifts "from the City that is built four-square."

Insulated as he was, by grief at the death of loved ones and by retirement from public life, his natural bent toward the fairest strengthened. The peace of the hills led him higher. "Seeing beyond, time is a little thing!" So sang the poet in 1912. He feels the sorrows and defeats of life merge and quickly lose themselves in the greatness of eternity. Thus eternity comes to him often. In anxiety and doubt does not the strain of hope rise higher than the note of fear? Is not this a "vision of the after-while"? the Perfect City that

> . . . lies so near that often in the dawn,
>> Or when the stars first show their silver fire,
>>> We seem on old lost ways we once have trod:
>> Upon the grass a Light no more withdrawn,
>>> Upon the wind a Song time cannot tire,
>>>> And in our hearts the very Voice of God.[6]

Friends, similarly, stand in the light of the Perfect City. A loved one is "the symbol and the seal of dreams eternal." Visioning peace, rest, hope, joy, and light here, in death his friends are the hope of Reality beyond. Of Lionel Johnson and Walter Pater, both of happy influence, he sings with this assurance:

> Sweet ministers throughout my troubled days,
>> Proof of my hope, and what at last shall be,—
>>> White souls, wrapped round in everlasting peace.[7]

And of other friends lost in death, he feels a presence. Have they, perchance, come down from the heights to strengthen the faith of his loving heart that those who have gone before will be near in that dread moment of the end? Be that as it may, he believes that in death at least they will await him, "crowned with the roses of eternity." And, still consistently, loving nature, beauty, wonder, vision, and friends with a love that Heaven cannot reject, his constant soul mounts above any disturbing doubt and

> Turns ever to the unknown land where lies
>> The white immortal City of its dreams—[8]

where dwell his friends, the Lovers of the Light.

The perfection of the Beauty that Thomas S. Jones, Jr.,
sought in life was Truth. It was Truth in its shining
sanctity. To quote his vision:

> . . . so pure, so high
> Is Truth; so rarely seen, a swift glance fills
> The soul with radiance, as when the frail
> New moon's white shadow lights a fading sky.[9]

That "splendor veritatis" the poet apprehended in the
Godhead, the Beginning and End of the perfection that he
sought. He saw it, too, in all those who prefigured and
followed the God-Man, Christ, the Perfect Lover. Singing,
then, the fullness of a heart seeking the fairest and burning
with the intensity of white flame, he celebrated in song,
mystery and miracle, vision and revelation.

"Let Faith's pure light Flame from the holy altar in thy
heart." Before he sang those lines, he had set up in his
heart an altar where burned the flame of his lively faith.
He kept alive the flame with lyric love. Through Eckhart
the Mystic, he sings the primal mystery of Love: the wonder
of the Trinity. Through this Lover of the Light, he says,

> Men hear of Him that angels cannot name,
> In Whom the Light, the Word, the Breath are One,[10]

and therein comprehend the mystery of Unity. Creation's
birth the poet renews through Caedmon's inspired song;
man's trust in God bears witness to Love, Justice, and
Providence as the attributes of the Creator: "For all His
Ways are infinitely just, And like a star His Love will lead
thee Home." And recalling the great sacrifice, the first
"Fiat" uttered by the God-Man, there remains for one, in
the face of darkness, doubt, fear, and blinding beauty,

> To find in God a final resting place—
> Refuge beneath the Shadow of His Wings.[11]

Overshadowing the other attributes of God is His Love. His is the Voice of Love. It urges the soul on to Himself, the Author of Perfection, the Law of Beauty and of Light. Through the ways of time, it pursues the soul to conformity to His Holy Will. It comes from the path of the stars: these words of God, like vast beams of light sending out their rays to other planets and then returning to the earth to stay.

"The Spirit and the Law" is a purely Christian chant: Christ, the fulfillment of the Law and the Prophets, and, consequently, the Redeemer of fallen man. Apart from historical research that Christ established a New Law, is the testimony of the Evangelists witnessing His intention to

> "remove the barrier that separates Jew from Gentile, that there will be but one shepherd and one flock."

The poem identifies Christ as the prophet like unto Moses. On "lone mountain sides," it places Moses roughly tracing laws which until the end of time will mould men's conscience, and,

> Then another, He Whose tender art
> Moved multitudes to seek through time and space
> The brooding love that craves a dwelling place
> Within the mystery of the human heart.[12]

Again, the poet heralds the plan of Redemption in the prerogative of the Son of God to effect a reconciliation between His Eternal Father and man lost to Paradise. He shows us Earth in her maternal solicitude sustaining her offspring for the prolonged existence of "a little hour"; Eve, the Mother of the Living, whose guilt atoned draws us back as weary pilgrims to "The garden gained by piteous Calvary": and lastly, Mary who, "alone immune," could answer the angel's salutation to be Eve's Reparatrix and so share in the Redemption. Invoking Mary as

O Holy Mother of the Incarnate Word,
    Who gave white Christmas to a world's despair,
        We kneel to thee, the Lily of death's vale,[13]

he revisions the Canticle of Canticles: "Nigra sum sed formosa, filiae Jerusalem." This mystery of Love he sings again in this quatrain:

Girdled by glittering stars no mind can span,
    A spark among the silver galaxies,
    Lift upon high, dark earth, show unto these
The wonder of all worlds—the Son of Man.[14]

The Public Life of the Master the poet celebrates in the ecstasy of Thabor when the favored three saw the Christ transfigured on the mountain-top and, thereafter, like Mary, kept in their heart the vision and pondered over it, or, as the sonnet sings:

Like a pearl we hold
Close to our hearts what we have heard and seen.[15]

The motif of Holy Week is in the octave of "Jerusalem." In fulfillment of the prophecy of Isaiah, the Master passed amid the Hosannas of a multitude which within six days would clamor for his crucifixion. He Who had worked miracles on men's bodies and souls, He

Whose Love was greater than the Ancient Law
Rides to His death beyond the city gate,[16]

pays the price of original sin and teaches men the beautiful lesson of universal charity:

Immortally He pardons your dark sin:
Forgive them for they know not what they do.[17]

Christ's Divinity Thomas S. Jones, Jr. evidences in the revelation of Spring when through the air blow silver trumpets announcing

> He is not far, the bright, the Risen God—
> Cleave but the wood and lift the sun-drenched stone.[18]

Stressing the supreme love of the God-Man, the poet reverts to the tradition that Christ, in tribute to the Virgin of Virgins, first presents the vision of His glorified Presence to His Mother. Further love he traces as he follows to Emmaus the two disciples who had witnessed the miracle of the Resurrection, but whose eyes were held that they should not recognize the Master until He broke the Bread with them and then

> . . . there seemed
> A light upon them, though the day was dead;
> They saw then Who had journeyed by their side
> Only to lose Him—and each thought he dreamed:
> But on the table lay the broken bread.[19]

Adhering to Revelation still, Thomas S. Jones, Jr., interprets the last mystery of Christ as Man: His Ascension into Heaven, the complete consummation of Infinite Love. Here is the sonnet:

> That He might better of Love's mystery tell
> Into a lonely mountain they withdrew;
> Day's golden fire cooled in deep wells of dew
> About His Head with softened splendor fell;
> And in each heart that heard the last farewell
> A quickening joy and deepening sorrow grew,
> And all were hushed—even the doubtful knew
> His was the power of Heaven and of Hell.
>
> When He has ceased, a mighty wind rushed by
> From far beyond the sunset's cloudless rim,
> And over them a glory seemed to bend;

Then like a star He rose into the sky,
   Sadly they watched the glowing light grow dim
   And heard the echoes ring, "Until the End."[20]

With Christ ascended into Heaven, the poet turns to
all lovers of the Light, those who burned with a "white
desire for God." And so he sings of David, the Shepherd
King and precursor of Christ, of Solomon, the builder of
the Temple, of Ezekiel, who foretold the destruction of the
Temple, and Isaiah "who prophesied the true Temple," to
quote the poet. That Temple was "By God begotten, yet
the Son of Man." Here is belief in the two natures of
Christ. With the prophets he places the philosophers.
Prior to the advent of Christ, the convictions of these
high-priests of thought, whether pagan or Christian in
philosophy, centre on the God-Man as the cardinal principle of life. "Akhnaton" professes faith, belief in God, as
the prerequisite for salvation:

   With Thy sweet Voice throughout eternity
   Call on my name and it shall never fail.

Zarathustra rehearses the power of the Son of Light to
draw the Magi to His side; Pythagoras, through his theory
of numerical combinations, is led to Unity—God; Seneca
acknowledges Divinity and considers heavenly wisdom
above earth's affliction: "What wisdom hallows death cannot destroy"; and Plato's *Idea* resolves into God Himself
from Whom all things come and to Whom all return:

   And through the shadows that the God had drawn
      From His immortal substance, Plato saw
      Beauty to which all Being shall return.

But those most radiant in the white light of the Perfect
City are the Saints. They are the Light-Bringers. Whether
the poet sings of the Doctors, the Fathers of the Church,

the martyrs, or the missionaries, he does so with an intimacy that is almost kinship: it was the climax of his search
for perfection. And moving in this Kingdom of Divine
Love, he maintained his mood. He championed the Saints,
celebrating their vision, their revelations, and their
miracles.

He calls "The coming of the Saints, the golden days!"
They mean the Christianizing of Britain when the faint
strains of Druidism were lost in the prayers around the
holy wells of curing power. Pictish kings are shadowed
by the figure of the Cross. Druid bards are silent before
the white-cowled monks,

> Saints with unshod feet
> Who had the strength to pray, the faith to do.[21]

Men like Kevin, Brendan, Oran, Columba, Aidan, Oswald,
and Cuthbert face heathen hordes, speak God's name, light
the flame of chivalry, and then behold "The Vision sought
by dreams of men." Bride is the Mary of the Gael; Enda,
the sacred and educative influence on Aran Mor; Cadoc,
Illtyd, Benedict, Augustine, Hilda, Boniface, Queen Margaret, and Columcille are angels who go in Love's defence
to preach the Word. They symbolize to him those who
have left all that they may find all. They give "The perfect
service without recompense." Bernard is the Crusader
fired with zeal to kindle the flame of chivalry to war for
the Cross. Yet, in the cry of the liegemen advancing to the
Holy City, the poet would have the Saint hear that minor
strain calling to the heart of men in succeeding ages that
the conquest of the far Jerusalem, the Perfect City, is made

> By him who slays the self with ghostly sword,
> Who holds within his breast Christ's Sepulchre.[22]

The pure heart, "Christ's Sepulchre," the poet celebrates in frequent verse. To him it was the efficacy of a prayer from such ageless innocence that made the words of Julian of Norwich "reveal the largess Love will shower"; that made the dust in Gregory's hand blossom "with blood-drops redder than a rose"; that inspired the choice of Dunstan as ruler of Glastonbury; that favored Isidore with the assistance of angels; that moved the Christ-Child to accept the offering of the little Herman Joseph; that made earth blossom beneath the feet of Francis; and that led the angels to fold Chad's soul "Within the silver circle of their wings."

With equal ardor he renews the love-deeds of the Saints in verse: the miracle of Bega's veil, the heavenly roses wrought through the charity of Elizabeth, the flowering of the Holy Thorn at Christmastide, the flight of Scholastica's soul to Heaven, the victory of Clovis urged on by the saintly Clotilda, the Presence of Christ in place of the beggar to whom Martin had given his cloak. Often he sings the Miracle of the Host, as when St. Genevieve bade the liegemen "bear Christ's Body, till they felt mid stark despair a King's high Presence guard their citadel." Clare, too, disbands her foemen as she stands with the "lifted Host, the heavenly Bread."

Next upon his calendar of perfection, the poet places the Scholastics: Saint Bonaventura, the Angelic Doctor, whose book was the image of the Crucified; Thomas of Aquin, who knew all learning that was known to man but who sought beyond the wisdom of the earth searching for

> . . . Love's dwelling-place;
> Till in the Host where life has mystic birth
> He saw the God Who gave the Wine and Bread
> Unveil the hidden beauty of His Face.[23]

Akin to Aquinas, the Patron of the Schools, is his teacher,

the Dominican philosopher, theologian, and scientist, who, through his learning, found that Love alone can bring the hearts of men unto Itself.

Nearest to the Heart of Perfection are the Mystics: Francis of Assisi, Eckhart and his disciple, Henry Suso, whose style was warmed and colored with the purely orthodox; Blessed John Ruysbroeck, the foremost of the Flemish Mystics; the valiant Teresa favored even to the transverberation of her ecstatic heart; and John of the Cross, who like Teresa, made

> Sublime surrender, perfect gift of gifts:
> . . . .
> With stern eyes fixed upon Infinity—
> Godhead! that holds the height and depth of Love.[24]

Nor does the poet venerate only early Christian times in his work. He gives maiden tribute in poetry to those heroes of love, lately canonized followers of Ignatius, who renounced the shelter of the cloister in Knighthood for the Cross. In a virgin land they spent themselves that

> Love might sway
> One heart among a dark barbaric race.[25]

Noel de Sillery, Jean de Brebeuf, Isaac Jogues, Paul le Jeune, and the other North American Martyrs dream of Christ amid the howls of wolves, the Mohawk host, and their "whining bowstrings." Now the poet sees them in the Perfect City: "Heroes on heights invisible they stand."

He celebrates the early scientists: Copernicus, Tycho Brahe, Galileo, Spinoza, and Pascal, who conceived great laws in nature, yet beyond the phenomena traced in love and reverence for the truth, "The stern and austere outline of the Cross"; the artists: Michelangelo, Da Vinci, the architect of "dreamlike cities," Angelico, whose beauty of soul pictures Paradise "for a gray world," Giotto, Botticelli, who paints "A home in which his haunted soul may rest" are human symbols to the poet of Invisible Truth.

Singing the Perfect City through the perfection of beauty in nature and in man through his angel stature and closeness to God, Thomas S. Jones, Jr., pays tribute to earth's fairest creature and Heaven's Queen. Evesham was built, he sings, as a bower for the "Queen whose brow by seven stars was bound." Walter of Bierbeeke enlisted in the tournament as the Knight of Mary. Albertus Magnus kept a holy tryst with her. Fra Angelico painted her. Love places her image upon "the crystal capes of Labrador." The poet, seeing Mary as the symbol of the whitest splendor, the quest and the attainment of his own pure heart, calls her "Pale, blossomed-crowned, Our Lady of the May." And always she is the Virgin-Mother.

"Singer of the Perfect City," Thomas S. Jones, Jr., sees Love as the unifying force to bring men unto the Divine Ideal. It is the "Summa" of his work; it is the "Summa" of his belief. In a letter to the writer, he has said:

> There is a mystery in the spirit of the true saint, mystic, and poet. "Blessed are the pure in heart." This insight is God's gift, and not understood in the world. It is not apprehended by the reason or the desire. The Church of the Saints is only won through love: reason and intellectual processes have nothing to do with it.

God's Love created and opened Heaven for the happiness of man. Mary's love kept her the Virgin-Mother. The Saints moved in Love because, as the poet says, it "is the Kingdom of the Holy Ghost." Through the testament of Love that the God-Man has left men, in all the passing ages they may kneel "before Love's very Presence." Love, too, he knows has let man commune with the blessed in the Perfect City,

for like "celestial messengers, tired souls befriending" they
share the merits of their deeds on earth with those who seek
their aid. Through John, the Apostle of Love, who saw in
revelation Heaven open at the Will of Love, Thomas S.
Jones, Jr. proclaims his *Vale* to the world. It is the Voice
that spoke to him first from the silences, that lifted him to
seek Infinity. It is the message of the "Fourth Gospel":

> The sea's great voices into silence blend
>> And dawn's vermilion peaks are hushed to hear
> The Voice of Love that casts out every fear
And calls its creatures to their ordered end:
As scattered flames in one bright arc ascend
>> To find the center of the golden sphere,
>> In seraph-splendor sons of earth draw near,
Loved to the loving, friend to perfect friend.
>
> Here in the light of lonely skies and far,
>> Pale habitations of the spirit gleam,
>>> Old when the dayspring took his flaming throne;
> Here through the meadows of the Morning Star
>> Falls the faint music heard within a dream—
>> The Lover's accents calling to His Own.[26]

ONE WORD MORE

POETRY, true poetry, has, we have seen, always been sincere. Poets, true poets, have always striven to express their deep and heartfelt conclusions about the existence in which they find themselves. This pursuit of truth, of the meaning of existence, has been evident in the poetry of every century. The nineteenth century, with its variety of philosophies: rationalism, materialism, agnosticism, transcendentalism, and Darwinism, particularly harassed its poets. The current century, which is the offspring of this confusion, and whose paganism has increased it, stands even deeper in the shadow.

In these pages we have tried to discover what is the attitude of some present-day poets toward the relationship of man's heart with his Creator. Here, as always, there are men who walk in almost utter darkness, some who seek only to push aside a single cloud to reach the full light of the sun, and some who receive the light in direct rays.

Those who walk in almost utter darkness we have called "Lovers of Earthly Beauty": pagans who have a distorted knowledge of the Being they call God. How many of them verify the saying of wisdom that in his heart no man thinks there is no God! One denies the existence of Deity and later celebrates in a jubilee poem the Father, the Son, and the Holy Ghost; another utters blasphemy and within the same poem chants a most exquisite tribute to the Holy Sacrifice of the Mass. In response to the craving for religion innate in their hearts, they acknowledge some kind of Supremacy; whether it be the One-Self of Wheelock; Fate, as defended by Masefield; Beauty, the god of Miss

Millay, the God of Elinor Wylie's stoic heart; or the God of Jeffers, the Deist.

Somewhat removed from these lovers of earth are the seekers after Truth. While all men are seekers, the poets in this class are confused, puzzled in their search. Blinded to the acceptance of any teaching church and of revelation, they grope their way alone, depending merely on human reason. Without the grace of revealed truth, without the guidance of an authority empowered to interpret truth, poets like Robinson, Markham, Lindsay, and Coffin must be puzzled ever.

Those who are certain of the existence in which they find themselves we call "Poets Naturally Christian." One might go farther and call them "Poets Naturally Catholic." They abide by the Law of Love, which is the Universal Good, Love *semper, ubique, ab omnibus.* Alfred Noyes in the midst of scientific assurance of the nineteenth century saw it shine through the works of an Intelligent Creator and through it reached orthodoxy; T. S. Eliot felt it as he emerged from a miasmal mist of unbelief and doubt; Charles Williams celebrates it in its fundamentalism as nuptial love whereby it rises to the heights of the mysticism of Juliana of Norwich; Anna Hempstead Branch would bring its beneficence to all mankind; and Thomas S. Jones, Jr. has made it his *Vale* to a modern world.

NOTES

John Hall Wheelock: A Doubting Intellect and a Believing Heart

1. Wheelock, "The Man to His Dead Poet," *Dust and Light*, New York, Scribner, 1921, p. 168.
2. ——, "The Moonlight Sonata," ibid., p. 29.
3. ——, "A Meditation," *The Bright Doom*, New York, Scribner, 1927, p. 54.
4. ——, ibid., p. 52.
5. ——, "Ernest Dowson," *Dust and Light*, p. 118.
6. ——, "Tchaikovsky," *The Black Panther*, New York, Scribner, 1922, p. 35.
7. ——, "In the Dark City," ibid., p. 43.
8. ——, "The Undiscovered Country," *The Bright Doom*, p. 9.
9. ——, "Sea Voyage," ibid., p. 17.
10. ——, "Moonlight Sonata," *Dust and Light*, p. 29.
11. Wheelock, "Man to His Dead Poet," ibid., p. 165.
12. ——, "The Beloved," *The Black Panther*, p. 20.
13. ——, "Loneliness without End," *The Bright Doom*, p. 14.
14. ——, "Night Has Its Fear," *The Black Panther*, p. 7.
15. ——, ibid., p. 11.
16. ——, "Communion," *The Bright Doom*, p. 60.
17. ——, "Truce," ibid., p. 37.
18. ——, "Travail," *The Black Panther*, p. 28.
19. ——, "October Moonlight," ibid., p. 13.
20. ——, "Mirror," ibid., p. 36.
21. ——, "Tchaikovsky," ibid., p. 35.
22. ——, "The Years," *The Bright Doom*, p. 62.
23. ——, "This Quiet Dust," ibid., p. 15.

Edna St. Vincent Millay Revels in Her Love of Earth

1. Millay, "Moriturus," *The Buck in the Snow*, New York, Harper, 1928, p. 7.
2. F. T. Wood, "On the Poetry of John Masefield," *The Poetry Review*, May-June, 1933, p. 199.
3. Millay, "Afternoon on a Hill," *Renascence*, New York, Kennerly, 1927, p. 41.
4. Millay, "Passer Mortuus Est," *Second April*, New York, Harper, 1921, p. 23.
5. ——, "Prayer to Persephone," ibid., p. 70.
6. ——, "Sonnet III," ibid., p. 79.

7. Millay, "Sonnet XIII," "The Harp Weaver," New York, Harper, 1923, p. 65.
8. ——, "Moriturus," *The Buck in the Snow,* p. 9.
9. ——, "The Anguish," ibid., p. 31.
10. ——, "To Jesus on His Birthday," ibid., p. 67.
11. ——, "Sonnet XXVI," *Fatal Interview,* New York, Harper, 1931, p. 26.
12. Millay, "Sonnet XIV," ibid., p. 14.
13. ——, "Sonnet LII," ibid., p. 52.
14. ——, "Sonnet XXIX," ibid., p. 29.
15. ——, "Moriturus," *The Buck in the Snow,* p. 7.

Elinor Wylie: Toward the Light

1. Wylie, "Letter to V—," *Collected Poems,* New York, Knopf, 1932, p. 302.
2. ——, "The Lie," ibid., p. 228.
3. ——, "The Viennese Waltz," ibid., p. 255.
4. ——, "The Loving Cup," ibid., p. 231.
5. ——, "Fire, Sleet, and Candlelight," ibid., p. 28.
6. ——, "Farewell, Sweet Dust," ibid., p. 221.
7. ——, "Innocent Landscape," ibid., p. 123.
8. ——, "Where, O Where," ibid., p. 153.
9. ——, "Song," ibid., p. 52.
10. ——, "Drowned Woman," ibid., p. 53.
11. Wylie, "Unwilling Admission," ibid., p. 154.
12. ——, "Indentured," ibid., p. 291.
13. ——, "Felo de Se," ibid., p. 198.
14. ——, "A Courtesy," ibid., p. 273.
15. ——, "Sanctuary," ibid., p. 14.
16. ——, "Valentine," ibid., p. 41.
17. ——, "Absent Thee from Felicity Awhile," ibid., p. 196.
18. ——, "Full Moon," ibid., p. 47.
19. ——, "This Corruptible," ibid., p. 204.
20. ——, ibid.
21. ——, "Birthday Sonnet," ibid., p. 311.
22. ——, "Singing Girl," ibid., p. 102.
23. ——, "Birthday Sonnet," ibid., p. 311.

John Masefield: Poet of a Mercy Everlasting

1. Masefield, "Shakespeare and Spiritual Life," *The Romanes Lecture.* 1924.
2. Masefield, ibid.
3. ——, "Sonnets," *Poems,* p. 370. New York, Macmillan, 1929.

4. Masefield, "The Widow in the Bye Street," ibid., p. 156.
5. ——, "Shakespeare and Spiritual Life," *The Romanes Lecture.*
6. ——, "Right Royal," *Poems,* Pt. II, p. 213. New York, Macmillan, 1928.
7. ——, ibid., p. 214.
8. ——, "Enslaved," ibid., p. 96.
9. ——, "Rosas," ibid., Pt. I, p. 426.
10. ——, "Lollingdon Downs," ibid., p. 404.
11. ——, "The Everlasting Mercy," ibid., p. 76.

12. Masefield, "The Widow in the Bye Street," ibid., p. 191.
13. ——, "The Everlasting Mercy," ibid., p. 76.
14. ——, "Lollingdon Downs," ibid., p. 400.
15. ——, "The Everlasting Mercy," ibid., p. 92.
16. ——, "Lollingdon Downs," ibid., p. 402.
17. ——, "Sonnets," ibid., p. 359.
18. ——, "Sonnets," ibid., p. 347.
19. ——, ibid.
20. ——, ibid., p. 357.

ROBINSON JEFFERS Takes God to Task

1. Jeffers, "Thurso's Landing," *Thurso's Landing,* New York, Liveright, 1932, p. 91.
2. ——, "Still the Mind Smiles," *Give Your Heart to the Hawks,* New York, Random House, 1933, p. 115.
3. ——, "Give Your Heart to the Hawks," ibid., pp. 91-92.
4. ——, "The Women at Point Sur," *The Women at Point Sur,* New York, Liveright, 1927, p. 101.
5. ——, ibid., p. 33.
6. ——, ibid., p. 101.
7. ——, ibid., p. 49.
8. ——, ibid., p. 26.
9. ——, ibid., p. 86.

10. Jeffers, ibid., p. 33.
11. ——, "In the Hill at New Grange," *Give Your Heart to the Hawks,* p. 132.
12. ——, "Intellectuals," ibid., p. 113.
13. ——, "The Women at Point Sur," *The Women at Point Sur,* p. 78.
14. ——, ibid., p. 36.
15. ——, ibid., p. 121.
16. ——, "Dear Judas," *Dear Judas,* New York, Liveright, 1929, p. 34.
17. ——, ibid., p. 35.
18. ——, ibid.
19. ——, "Birth Dues," ibid., p. 121.

EDWIN ARLINGTON ROBINSON: The First of the Seekers

1. Robinson, "Matthias at the Door," *Matthias at the Door*, p. 93, New York, Macmillan, 1931.
2. ——, *The Glory of the Nightingales*, p. 35, New York, Macmillan, 1930.
3. ——, "Matthias at the Door," *Matthias at the Door*, p. 59.
4. ——, ibid., p. 68.
5. ——, "Talifer," *Talifer*, p. 35, New York, Macmillan, 1933.
6. ——, "Ponce de Leon," *Nicodemus*, p. 40, New York, Macmillan, 1932.
7. ——, *The Glory of the Nightingales*, p. 39.
8. ——, *Amaranth*, p. 55, New York, Macmillan, 1934.
9. ——, "Sonnet," *Sonnets*, p. 27, New York, Macmillan, 1928.
10. ——, "Octave XXII," *Collected Poems*, p. 107, New York, Macmillan, 1925.
11. Robinson, "Two Quatrains," ibid., p. 108.
12. ——, "L'Envoi," *Collected Poems*, p. 108.
13. ——, "Calvary," *Sonnets*, p. 1.
14. ——, "Tasker Norcross," *Collected Poems*, p. 500.
15. ——, *The Glory of the Nightingales*, p. 17.
16. ——, *Cavender's House*, p. 26, New York, Macmillan, 1929.
17. ——, "The Laggards," *Sonnets*, p. 83.
18. ——, *Cavender's House*, p. 69.
19. ——, *The Glory of the Nightingales*, p. 69.
20. ——, "Matthias at the Door," *Matthias at the Door*, p. 87.
21. ——, *The Glory of the Nightingales*, p. 23.
22. ——, *Amaranth*, p. 86.
23. ——, *Cavender's House*, p. 19.

VACHEL LINDSAY Chants a Gospel of Rapture for Mankind

1. Lindsay, "Proclamation of the Gospel of Beauty," a broadside sent the writer by the poet.
2. ——, "For All Who Ever Sent Lace Valentines," *Collected Poems*, p. 65, New York, Macmillan, 1930.
3. Lindsay, "The Beggar's Valentine," ibid., p. 299.
4. ——, ibid., p. 299.
5. ——, "The Illinois Village," ibid., p. 74.
6. ——, "On the Building of Springfield," ibid., p. 75.

7. Lindsay, "The Town of American Visions," ibid., p. 347.

8. ——, "The Springfield of the Far Future," ibid., p. 348.

9. ——, "The Immaculate Conception Church," ibid., p. 306.

10. ——, ibid., p. 307.

11. ——, "The Star of My Heart," ibid., p. 307.

12. ——, "Foreign Missions in Battle Array," ibid., p. 338.

13. ——, "Litany of the Heroes," ibid., p. 190.

14. ——, "The Sun Says His Prayers," ibid., p. 68.

15. Lindsay, "How a Little Girl Danced," ibid., p. 64.

16. ——, "The Celestial Circus," ibid., p. 286.

17. ——, "King Arthur's Men Have Come Again," ibid., p. 336.

18. ——, "Simon Legree," ibid., pp. 162, 163.

19. ——, "The Hope of the Resurrection," ibid., p. 278.

20. ——, "Where is the Real Non-Resistant," ibid., p. 390.

EDWIN MARKHAM: Prophet of a Kingdom Coming

1. Markham, "My Creed," *The New Church Messenger*, March 5, 1930.

2. ——, Lecture at Bowdoin St. Church, Boston, Feb. 2, 1930.

3. ——, "Little Brothers of the Ground," *The Man with the Hoe*, New York, Doubleday, Doran, 1929, p. 24.

4. ——, "The Angelus," *Lincoln and Other Poems*, New York, Doubleday, Doran, 1928, p. 42.

5. ——, "Field Fraternity," ibid., p. 50.

6. ——, "The Muse of Labor," ibid., p. 62.

7. ——, "The Leader of the People," ibid., p. 55.

8. ——, "The Desire of Nations," *The Man with the Hoe*, p. 35.

9. ——, "A Creed," "Lincoln and Other Poems," p. 25.

10. Markham, "The Witness of the Dust," ibid., p. 22.

11. ——, "The Christ of the Andes," *The Gates of Paradise*, New York, Doubleday, Doran, 1928, p. 61.

12. ——, "Ghosts in Flight," ibid., p. 71.

13. ——, "Peace Over Earth Again," ibid., p. 87.

14. ——, "The Heart's Cry," *New Poems*, New York, Doubleday, Doran, 1932, p. 46.

15. ——, "Immortable," ibid., p. 67.

16. ——, "Bridals Beyond," ibid., p. 50.

17. ——, "If He Should Come," ibid., p. 93.

18. ——, "Brotherhood," *The Man with the Hoe*, p. 21.

Robert P. Tristram Coffin Finds Faith in the Flash of a Heron's Wing

1. Coffin, "Rura Cano," *The Yoke of Thunder*, New York, Macmillan, 1929, p. 4.
2. ——, ibid.
3. ——, "A Whippoorwill Awakes," ibid., p. 33.
4. ——, "Rura Cano," ibid., p. 6.
5. ——, "Crystal Moment," ibid., p. 8.
6. ——, "Fireflies," ibid., p. 10.
7. ——, "Nothing Changes with the Birds," ibid., p. 35.
8. ——, "When Man Hung a Scythe," ibid., p. 39.
9. ——, "The Ram," *The Golden Falcon*, New York, Macmillan, 1929, p. 39.
10. ——, "The Barnacles," *The Yoke of Thunder*, p. 45.
11. ——, "The Jelly Fish," ibid., p. 46.
12. ——, "Now in the Hive," *Strange Holiness*, New York, Macmillan, 1936, p. 55.
13. Coffin, "There Is No Help in Bees," *The Yoke of Thunder*, p. 56.
14. ——, "The Older Love," ibid., p. 89.
15. ——, "Wild Geese at Night," ibid., p. 61.
16. ——, "St. Brandan of the West," *Dew and Bronze*, New York, A. & C. Boni, 1927, p. 29.
17. ——, "The Night Watchman," *The Yoke of Thunder*, p. 60.
18. ——, "The Spider," *The Golden Falcon*, p. 41.
19. ——, "A Buck's Head on the Wall," *The Yoke of Thunder*, p. 15.
20. ——, "The Heron," *The Golden Falcon*, p. 38.
21. ——, "Song for March," *The Yoke of Thunder*, p. 64.

T. S. Eliot Emerges from the Waste Land

1. Eliot, "Gerontion," *Collected Poems*, 1909-1925, New York, Harcourt, Brace, 1928, p. 50.
2. ——, "The Fire Sermon," ibid., p. 101.
3. ——, "Ash Wednesday" I., *Ash Wednesday*, New York, Putnam, 1930, p. 13.
4. Eliot, ibid., p. 14.
5. ——, ibid., p. 15.
6. ——, "Ash Wednesday" III., ibid., p. 21.
7. ——, "Ash Wednesday" IV., ibid., p. 22.
8. ——, "Ash Wednesday" VI., ibid., p. 27.

9. Eliot, ibid., p. 29.
10. ——, "Ash Wednesday" II., ibid., p. 18.
11. ——, *Journey of the Magi*, London, Faber and Gwyer, 1927, p. 2.

12. Eliot, *A Song for Simeon*, ibid., 1928, p. 2.
13. ——, "Animula," *Animula*, London, Faber & Faber, 1929, p. 1.

ALFRED NOYES: Balladist and Oarsman of God

1. Noyes, *The Unknown God*, p. 34. New York, Sheed and Ward, 1934.
2. ——, "Mist in the Valley," *Collected Poems*, New York, Stokes, 1913. Vol. II, p. 3.
3. ——, *The Unknown God*, p. 96. New York, Sheed and Ward, 1934.
4. ——, "The Sacred Oak," *The Lord of Misrule*, p. 116. New York, Stokes, 1915.
5. ——, "The Open Door," *Collected Poems*, Vol. III, p. 186. New York, Stokes, 1913.
6. ——, "A Post Impression," ibid., Vol. I, p. 77.
7. ——, "The Origin of Life," ibid., Vol. I, p. 87.
8. ——, ibid.
9. ——, ibid.
10. ——, "On the Death of Francis Thompson," ibid., Vol. II, p. 73.

11. Noyes, "The Old Sceptic," ibid., Vol. I, p. 58.
12. ——, "The Sailor King," ibid., Vol. II, p. 118.
13. ——, "The Optimist," ibid., Vol. I, p. 76.
14. ——, "Resurrection," ibid., Vol. II, p. 78.
15. ——, "The Testimony of Art," ibid., p. 76.
16. ——, "To the Pessimists," ibid., Vol. III, p. 286.
17. ——, "The Avenue of the Allies," ibid., pp. 140-141.
18. ——, "The Victorious Dead," ibid., p. 221.
19. ——, "Michael Oaktree," ibid., p. 298.
20. ——, "Paraclete," *The Lord of Misrule*, p. 74.
21. ——, "The Trumpet of the Law," *Collected Poems*, Vol. III, p. 75.

Charles Williams Sings the Mystery of Love

1. Williams, "Ode for Easter Morning," *Poems of Conformity*, London, Oxford University Press, 1920, p. 12.
2. ——, ibid., p. 121.
3. ——, "Ecclesia Docere," ibid., p. 49.
4. ——, "Orthodoxy," ibid., p. 48.
5. ——, "Presentation," ibid., p. 46.
6. ——, "To Michal: after a Vigil," *Divorce*, p. 27.
7. ——, "Sonnets XII," *Poems of Conformity*, p. 41.
8. ——, "To Michal Meditating a New Costume," *Divorce*, London, Oxford University Press, p. 69.
9. ——, "Ballade of Travelers," ibid., p. 22.
10. Williams, "At the Gates," ibid., p. 43.
11. ——, "Politics," ibid., p. 47.
12. ——, "Dialogue between Republic and the Apostasy," p. 40.
13. ——, ibid., p. 42.
14. ——, "Commentaries III," *Poems of Conformity*, p. 58.
15. ——, "Commentaries V," ibid., p. 61.
16. ——, "Christmas," *Divorce*, p. 95.
17. ——, "The Assumption," *Poems of Conformity*, p. 86.
18. ——, "Pentecost," ibid., p. 102.
19. ——, "Black Letter Days," ibid., p. 64.

Anna Hempstead Branch: Lover of Man and of the Mystic

1. Branch, "Divinity," *The Heart of the Road*, Boston, Houghton Mifflin, 1901, p. 29.
2. ——, "Sonnet in the Night," ibid., p. 23.
3. ——, "Haunted," ibid., p. 25.
4. ——, ibid., p. 25.
5. ——, "While Loveliness Goes By," *The Shoes That Danced*, Boston, Houghton Mifflin, 1915, p. 60.
6. ——, "Shame on Thee, O Manhattan," ibid., p. 67.
7. Branch, "To a New York Shop-Girl Dressed for Sunday," ibid., pp. 70-72.
8. ——, "Sonnet," *Sonnets from a Lock Box*, Boston, Houghton Mifflin, 1929, p. 12.
9. ——, "Sonnet XXIX," ibid., p. 31.
10. ——, "Sonnet XXXII," ibid., p. 34.
11. ——, "On a Bitter Cold Night," ibid., p. 68.
12. ——, ibid., p. 72.

13. Branch, "The Monk in the Kitchen," *Rose of the Wind*, p. 139.
14. ——, "Where No Thoughts Are," *The Heart of the Road*, p. 28.
15. ——, "A Vision in the Night," ibid., p. 98.
16. ——, "Pattern," *Sonnets from a Lock Box*, p. 117.
17. ——, "The Shoes That Danced," *The Shoes That Danced*, pp. 52-54.
18. ——, "To My Black Kitten," *Sonnets from a Lock Box*, p. 58.
19. ——, "The Thought of the Little Brother," *The Heart of the Road*, p. 6.
20. ——, "Inscription on the Christmas Candle," Christmas, 1934.
21. Branch, "To My Black Kitten," *Sonnets from a Lock Box*, p. 61.
22. ——, "Lazarus," *The Heart of the Road*, p. 62.
23. ——, "Rose of the Wind," *Rose of the Wind*, Boston, Houghton Mifflin, 1910, pp. 37-38.
24. ——, "Rose of the Wind," *Rose of the Wind*, p. 25.
25. ——, "In the Beginning," *Sonnets from a Lock Box*, p. 47.
26. ——, "Wild-wood Tree," ibid., p. 115.
27. ——, "Playing My Strange and Lovely Game," *Sonnets from a Lock Box*, p. 114.
28. ——, ibid.

THOMAS S. JONES, JR.: Singer of the Perfect City

1. Jones, "In Excelsis," *Shadow of the Perfect Rose*, New York, Farrar & Rinehart, 1937, p. 32.
2. ——, "At the White Gate," ibid., p. 41.
3. ——, "The Pines," ibid., p. 36.
4. ——, "The Gifts of Peace," ibid., p. 51.
5. ——, "The Rose Has Blown Away," ibid., p. 13.
6. ——, "Urbs Beata," ibid., p. 38.
7. ——, "On Lionel Johnson's Copy of Walter Pater's Gaston de Latour," ibid., p. 39.
8. ——, "The Hill-Top," ibid., p. 60.
9. ——, "Truth," ibid.
10. Jones, "Meister Eckhart," ibid., p. 172.
11. ——, "Refuge," ibid., p. 57.
12. ——, "The Spirit and the Law," ibid., p. 83.
13. ——, "The Three Mothers," ibid., p. 84.
14. ——, Unpublished quatrain.
15. ——, "According to St. Mark," ibid., p. 85.
16. ——, "Jerusalem," ibid., p. 85.
17. ——, ibid.
18. ——, Quatrain I, ibid., p. 65.
19. ——, "The Road to Emmaus," ibid., p. 86.
20. ——, "The Parting," ibid., p. 87.
21. ——, "Ciaran's City," ibid., p. 76.

22. Jones, "Saint Bernard," ibid., p. 165.

23. ——, "Saint Thomas Aquinas," p. 171.

24. ——, "Saint John of the Cross," ibid., p. 174.

25. Jones, "Tadousac," ibid., p. 185.

26. ——, "The Fourth Gospel," ibid., p. 148.